TWO MILLION MILES:

A Couple Goes Trucking

Dad from Mark & Kath

TWO MILLION MILES:

A Couple Goes Trucking

John & Virginia Logan

ISBN-13: 978-1466478404

Cover picture by Virginia Logan (see pp. 59-60)
Photography © by John and Virginia Logan
with the following exceptions:

Black-tailed Deer, U.S. Fish and Wildlife
Tree of Utah monument, U. S. Bureau of Land Management
U.S. Interstate map, U.S. Dept. of Transportation
John Day Dam, U.S. Army Corps of Engineers
Picture of Hyakutake, NASA
Geographic Center of the 50 U.S. States, USGS

The following photos are used by arrangement with Dreamstime:
Roadrunner
San Francisco Bay Bridge
Solar Halo
Magnifying a Washington D.C. map
Ambassador Bridge
California Poppies

Text Design and Publisher: Sara Leeland Books
                            www.saraleelandbooks.net
Cover Design by CreateSpace.com
Distribution through CreateSpace.com

Dedicated to

Marie and Jason,

Amelia & Sam;

and with thanks to
Jason for keeping our computer files up to date,
Marie for her encouragement to do the writing,
Elizabeth and Rosie for proofreading and suggestions,
and to Sara for bringing our writing into a book.

Two Million Miles:
A Couple Goes Trucking

Contents

TRUCKING TERMS

Big Hook: A tow truck capable of hooking up a 5-axle truck

Bobtailing: Driving tractor without trailer

Deadheading: Driving without a paying load in the
          trailer

Dispatch: Orders for pickup and delivery

Feathering: Using a very gentle touch

Granny-gear: Lowest gear possible in transmission

Jake brake: A mechanism installed on diesel engines
          that, when activated, slows the vehicle.

Rig: The truck and trailer

The U. S. Interstate Road System: WEST

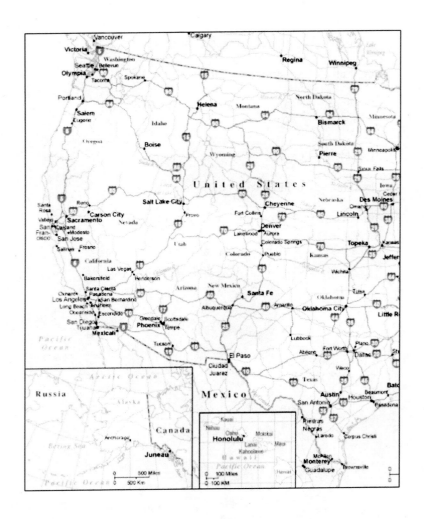

The U.S. Interstate Road System: EAST

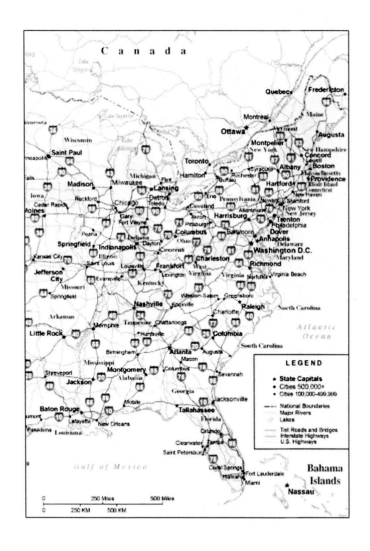

Virginia Logan receives her diploma and trucker's hat
at graduation from Eaton Truck Driving School,
Kalamazoo, MI

How We Got Into Trucking

Virginia Logan

When John was a young boy living in coal country, he watched the big trucks coming out of the mines and then hurtling down the curvy mountain roads. This is where his desire for trucking first started.

In his mid-twenties, he tried owning a semi-truck and driving, but got out before drowning in the expenses. Next, he tried dispatching with a freight company, and then moved on to manage freight sales. After many years of that cut-throat (while still partly enjoyable) existence, he was burned out and wanted something different.

He found that in driving a semi-truck for a logging company. He drove the company truck out into fields or wherever the logs were being cut, loaded up his truck and took the logs to a sawmill.

I went with him once to see the operation and also rode along on several trips delivering sawed boards to various businesses. John always said to me, "If I can do this driving, so can you."

I'd never thought about driving a truck, but, once our two children were grown, I was interested in a different kind of work than my office-based bookkeeping job.

So I signed up for a Truck Driving School course in Kalamazoo, Michigan. Taking evening classes meant stretching the course out for seven weeks. For those two months I worked all day at my office job in Grand Rapids, and then drove two hours down to the classes.

I was working full time at Western American Mailers right up until my first driving trip. I was also training a replacement. I'd finished the Eaton Driver School course in September, just before we signed on with Gainey Transportation (GTS or simply 'Gainey').

There were five people in this class and I was the only woman. Even today, only 6% of 3.2 million truckers are women. My first discovery was finding that I really enjoyed learning this new skill.

After successfully passing all the required testing, we signed up with Gainey Transportation in Grand Rapids, Michigan, a company that accepted training teams.

This is where our stories begin. At first, driving seemed simple. But read on to reach exciting chapters on mountain ice, urban tight spots and more adventures.

After a year and a half, we switched to Mill Creek, based in Holland, Michigan. Truckers say, "You have to make miles to make money," and we weren't getting enough miles with Gainey.

Note: John has always called me 'Jinny,' so in this book, Jinny and Virginia are the same person.

Virginia & John Logan
with their
Mill Creek truck

My First Long-Haul Run

John Logan

Jinny was still transitioning out of her office job when the opportunity for my training trip showed up. Gainey's best trainer for new teams, Big Mac, was in Grand Rapids and ready to go.

In spite of having worked in the trucking business for twenty years, I knew that going on the road as a long-haul trucker would be different. I had no experience at all with mountain driving.

We went to Herman Miller in Grandville, Michigan to hook up to our first load of office furniture. After doing the pre-trip inspection, we stopped at Holland's nearby Tulip City Truck Stop, a place on Gainey's list of best places to fuel.

There, we were joined by another driver, Pretty Boy. He was driving alone but said he intended to reach the West Coast as quickly as we two drivers did. I didn't see how he could. But, as this story unfolds, you'll see how it worked out.

I took the first shift out of Holland along the Lake Michigan shoreline, a road I'd driven hundreds of times. Driving past Chicago, however, I was in unfamiliar territory.

As we approached Peru, Illinois, Big Mac suggested that it was time for a stop and got on the CB to ask Pretty Boy where he wanted to pull in. Pretty Boy suggested the Big Red Coffee Pot in the Sky. That was a Sapp Brothers Truck Stop, with a big red pot logo—and some very good food on a 24 hour basis.

Then it was time for me to get some sleep. Big Mac had folded the top bunk down so that I could put a sleeping bag on it. I tried mightily to calm down inside a bag that was bouncing around in a noisy truck. The plan was to drive, then sleep, in 5-hour turns.

We pulled into the Flying J truck stop for food, and I called Jinny. I was excited and I think she was too.

I drove the next 5 hours, to Odessa, Nebraska, where Big Mac took the wheel until our fueling stop in Hillsdale, Wyoming. That Burns Brothers stop was popular, both for its food and for clean showers.

After Cheyenne, the highway started to climb. Cheyenne is 7,000 feet above sea-level. Laramie is the same. But to get from one to the other you must climb over Sherman Hill, an escarpment that goes up 1,640 feet in 40 miles. The rise is gradual, so only your popping ears tell you that you're gaining altitude.

At the summit of 8,640 feet, we passed a large statue of Lincoln's head (below) and started down a 10-mile grade 4 times as steep as the grade going up. Every mile took us down 164 feet. This was my first 'big truck' experience on a mountain grade.

Big Mac had coached me on how to handle it, explaining that key idea was 'control.' That meant *not* using the 'jake brake' (a special brake installed on diesel-engine trucks), but handling the steep grade using only engine gears and, very carefully, the air brakes.

If you used your brakes too hard they would heat up and fade (becoming useless to stop the truck) or, worse yet, catch on fire. Considerately, Big Mac pointed out marks showing where a truck had crashed just a week prior to our trip down this mountain!

My next test was to travel around Elk Mountain. Here the wind, as high as 70+ miles per hour, gets a shot at you. Then we'd be on Interstate 80 all the way to Rocklin, California, where our load was to be delivered.

I finished my shift at the Flying J in Rock Springs, Wyoming. Big Mac took over, driving on to Fort Bridger, a place built on the edge of three large steep hills, called the Three Sisters. No matter what the weather is like all the way across Wyoming, truckers say that it will always be terrible when you reach the Sisters.

We made it through Utah roads that took us past the beautiful Wasatch Mountains (picture below).

Then we descended into Red Rock Canyon, a valley filled with ranches and farms, with a trout stream wandering through its middle. The livestock, stream, trees, mountains and wildlife all added up to a 'most beautiful place.'

Next was the climb up to Parleys Summit, from which we could see another amazing vista. Bingo! As soon as we hit the summit, we started down an extremely steep grade, literally dropping right out of the sky and into the middle of Salt Lake City. I wasn't a bit tired anymore!

West of the Great Salt Lake, we stopped at Dell, Utah for fuel, and then headed for the Salt Flats, where the road is as straight as a taut string for about 55 miles. This salt-crusted land is flat for far enough that it's possible to actually see the curvature of the earth. Another moment of wonder!

At the west end of the flats, we crossed into Nevada and the town of Wendover. There, I got my first look at the inside of a real casino. The food was great and I even gambled a little bit. I didn't win, but I enjoyed the possibilities.

The very flat & white Salt Flats

After relaxing, I got back behind the wheel again, but not in Big Mac's truck. It had already become obvious why Pretty Boy wanted to run with our team. He went to bed while I drove his truck.

We had gone over four mountain passes when we came to Iron Point, a pass 5,280 feet high. I was rolling along ahead of Big Mac when he called on the radio. He said he had just lost his transmission. I told him I'd move over so he could come on down past me.

I drove Pretty Boy's truck on the shoulder as Big Mac came up in the left lane. He was cutting his speed by working his brakes, with no assist from his engine or gears. He flew by me like I was sitting still.

Pretty Boy must have had one ear open because he jumped right out of the bunk. I kept talking to Big Mac as he sped down the steep grade. Luckily, the road was fairly straight with only a couple of wide turns near the bottom.

It was dark and I could see a small town in the distance. I asked Big Mac if he could coast his truck to the little town.

He said he'd try, and we both made it to Goldconda, Nevada. Once he stopped, the transmission started to shift again. That was good because the only businesses in Goldconda were two bars and a small, closed gas station.

Big Mac decided he would make the rest of the run on the damaged transmission. I got back in with him and Pretty Boy drove his own truck from there. Big Mac was still driving as we crossed the state line into California, then up into the Sierra Mountains and over Donner Pass.

At the bottom of the mountain's west side was Rocklin, home to the Herman Miller Distribution Center, destination for our load. We dropped our trailer and headed for the Freightliner Dealer in Sacramento. They diagnosed the problem: the shifting fork inside the transmission was worn out.

We had two days in a motel while the transmission was fixed, a quiet end to one of the biggest adventures of my life.

Beginning Memories

Virginia Logan

Many of the early days in our trucking life are a chaotic blur in my memory, but, happily, my notes from that time are filled with details.

On my first trip, we picked up a load at Zeeland and headed for Rocklin, California. Our trainer, Big Mac, had just finished working with a team for 13 weeks without being sure that, even then, they were competent. His plan was to let the trainee start driving right away so that he could get a feel of what he was up against.

I had been riding with John to Chicago every Saturday for almost a year and even driving a little the last few months when I had my student Commercial Drivers License. So I was anxious to be able to drive right on through Chicago.

It had started to rain when Big Mac asked if I wanted to switch. I looked at him and indicated *not yet!* He looked at John and asked if he thought I could handle it and John said that if I thought I could, it was OK.

I drove. Because of the rain, it was a messy stop-and-go for many miles, but I made it past the toll gate to Minooka, Illinois—a whole 3 ½ hours.

Like John the week before, I was too excited to sleep. We were going to stop at Walcott, Iowa's I-80 Truck Stop, unique for its large Model-A truck at the entrance and for dozens of antique toy trucks and cars displayed in the restaurant and store.

After dinner, we continued on across Iowa and I easily fell asleep in the bunk. John & I had the bottom bunk, which is better for sleeping than the top bunk.

My next turn at driving was from Clive, Iowa to Grand Island, Nebraska. In Omaha there was a detour to follow because of construction. Big Mac was impressed that I just stayed calm, cool and collected *and* followed the detour signs. We made a quick switch at Grand Island. I hit the sack again and was out like a light.

Virginia on black rock at Black Rock Desert, Utah

John drove to Kimball, Nebraska where we switched again. We fueled and ate at Hillsdale, Wyoming and then I was to continue on up over Sherman Hill to Laramie.

It was a Wyoming October, and it started to snow on the mountain's east side. The thought that came into my head was: "Well, what would you do if you were just driving a car?" Answer: "Slow down, be careful and don't slam on the brakes." So I proceeded through the snow storm, around traffic, and up Sherman Hill.

Now it was time for the downhill. We had a fairly light load and so I was able to keep control quite easily. I went down into Laramie very slowly and continued on to the Bitter Creek Rest Area.

John drove from there, across Wyoming and into Utah. This time, he got to drive over Parley Summit and down into Salt Lake City. I was sound asleep, of course. It was many runs later before I actually saw this area in the daylight, and without fog. It ended up being one of my favorite places to drive through.

The next day Big Mac got on the phone to Gainey, saying that when we got back to Grand Rapids, we should have our own truck, because we didn't need more training. We were happy about that. We knew that Gainey had already accepted a load that we'd carry, going from Grand Rapids to Grand Prairie, Texas.

Golden Temple Granola Bars

John Logan

For the return half of our first trip together with Gainey's trainer, Big Mac, the dispatcher had told us to head north to Eugene, Oregon to pick up a load of granola bars for Ada, Michigan.

Jinny and Big Mac traded driving the truck north on Interstate 5. They passed Mount Shasta and continued on into the Siskiyou Mountains. I wasn't sleeping so I caught glimpses of the southern end of the volcanic Cascade Mountain Range.

Jinny was turning into what seemed like a natural mountain-driving trucker!

We stopped at a little truck stop nestled in between two mountains, where the food was good for picking up energy. It was not long before we were rolling into Eugene, Oregon. Big Mac called the shipper, Golden Temple, and discovered that the Grand Rapids purchase was by Amway Corporation to sell in their Health Foods Catalog.

The Golden Temple workers were all wearing an Indian head wrap, just like in the movies! We have since found many people in the northwestern states who wear that headgear. They were ready, so we were loaded up fast. They gave me a tasty granola bar just out of the oven.

We continued north on Interstate 5, running in a valley between two mountain ranges, the Coastal Range on our left and the Cascade Range on our right.

I was sticking my head out of the bunk quite often to catch the views. The next towns of any size were Corvallis and Salem, Oregon. There are lots of paper mill jobs in both towns. Salem is at the 45th Parallel, the halfway point between the Equator and the North Pole.

We reached Portland, Oregon, the Rose City. Because the Columbia River flows through the heart of the city, Portland is known not only for its roses, but also for its big bridges. It is common to see ocean-going ships loading and unloading right downtown, about 80 miles from the ocean.

In Portland, we turned east and drove along the Columbia River as it cuts its way through the Cascade Range. Volcanic lava towers thousands of feet above the river on both sides. Eastward were large dams, used to control the river and to generate electricity.

Columbia River, east of Portland

Not far up the river from Portland is Multnomah Falls. This waterfall has eaten a large cavity back into the mountainside. A small stream breaks over the edge of the mountain about 2000 feet up. It becomes a thin veil of water just falling and falling through the air, a natural beauty beyond words.

In the past, hundreds of people on the Oregon Trail died in their effort to reach this region. Settlers who got to Portland found rich farmland in a mild climate where just about anything would grow.

Continuing east, we could see snow-topped Mount Hood in the distance, its sides flanked by huge trees. Next we came to the Hood River area. The Columbia is very wide at this point and the walls of the valley go straight up from the sides of the river. This funnels the west wind into a relatively narrow valley with steep sides. Compressed between these walls, the wind gains strength. I have seen people here going at speeds on their sail boards that seem like flying on top of the water.

At The Dalles, Oregon, the valley is shallower. Huge sawmills and many aluminum production plants are located here. These last require a lot of electricity, and much of that comes from the Columbia River dams. Not far up-river, the John Day Dam (below) comes into view. Here water shoots out of the electricity generators and flies through the air in the direction of Interstate 84.

As we climbed out of the Columbia Valley, we drove into a large inland desert. Little rain falls here because the mountains to the west cut off the ocean's moisture.

At the eastern side of this desert you can see the Blue Mountains with their distinct blue cast. The city of Pendleton, Oregon, is here, home to Pendleton Woolen Goods. From up in the mountains, at night the city of Pendleton sparkles like a huge bowl full of jewels.

Life on the Road

Virginia Logan

The stories in this book range over the years from 1990 to 1997. GPS wasn't available then, so our route planning was done with paper maps, directions from our dispatcher and the receiver, or by getting tips over the CB radio from other truckers.

Cell phones weren't common until the late 1990s, so contact with our family while on the road was limited. In the last few years we had a 'bag phone.' It had a large battery and we had an antenna outside of the truck for better reception. Since cell towers weren't so common then, even its use was still not always reliable.

When we drove with Mill Creek, we had a satellite communications system. The satellite device was on the roof and we had a keyboard and monitor in the cab of the truck. With this system we could receive and send messages to our dispatcher at any time and they could also track where the truck was.

We were usually out on the road for 10 days to two weeks, then back home for two or three days to do our laundry, get mail, pay bills, and rest. Our longest time on the road was 3 weeks. Department of Transportation regulations limited driving to 10 hours for each driver within 24 hours. The 10 hours could be straight hours, or 5 driving and 5 'in the sleeper.' We usually chose the 5 /5 pattern. That left 4 hours a day for fueling and eating.

It was the drivers' responsibility to keep 'driver logs' up to date and correct.

We drove trucks belonging to the company (first Gainey, then Mill Creek) so each time we returned to home base, we always cleaned out the truck completely because we never knew when they might give the truck to someone else to drive. As a team we would get a new (or newer) truck at least once a year because we were putting a lot of miles on it.

The trailers we used had slots inside so that bars and straps could be used to secure loads. In most cases the trailers were loaded and unloaded by the customer, but in some cases we had to do it. We were only paid a flat fee of $25 regardless of how long it took. No matter who did the work, it was our responsibility to make certain the load was secure and wouldn't shift in transit.

Occasionally we would just be dropping a trailer at a location, but most often we would have a scheduled arrival time. We developed a reputation for dependable 'on time' arrivals. With the complications that could arise from traffic, weather, detours and unknown routes, being consistently 'on time' was a challenge and we took pride in meeting that challenge.

We were paid for the miles to the destination, not by the hour, so the incentive was always to make good time. We switched from Gainey to Mill Creek trucking because we found that we enjoyed the long haul trucking to the West Coast. Because long hauls had less time sitting around and waiting, they also paid better.

Everyone drives by truck weigh stations, but most don't know exactly what happens there. Usually we just drove the truck over the scales so the weigh master could check that we didn't exceed legal weights on steer axles, driver axles and trailer axles. The legal limit was 80,000 pounds for 5 axles.

The weigh master could also look the truck over and call us in for many reasons: lights, decals, permits. He can also do a more thorough check if he sees anything suspicious. He can put your truck out of service right there at the scales until you get the problem fixed.

Some states have a 'Port of Entry.' For example, when we started trucking, Wyoming's Port of Entry required that you go inside and show permits, then be given a 'horsey decal' that was to be displayed on the windshield while you were traveling across the state.

There are also agricultural and livestock inspection stations. Here we either had to show shipping documents or tell what our load was and where it came from. In the South, they would occasionally look for fire ants.

When we started trucking we tried an electric refrigerator in the truck in which we could carry meals. But we found that it was better to schedule regular stops to get out and eat at a restaurant. In the years that we did trucking, most of the big truck stops had real sit-down restaurants that served great food. Now it is pretty much all fast food.

We developed a list of favorite spots along various routes we typically traveled. For example, Sweetpea's in Arkansas had great barbecue ribs and a place in Gothenburg, Nebraska had awesome 'Platte Valley Berry Pie.' With much of our time spent sitting while driving, or sleeping, and little opportunity for exercise, it was a challenge to stay healthy.

People ask me what it was like to be a woman in the trucking business. As part of a team, I felt I was just out there doing a job. Single women truckers may have found it harder.

John and I went into this adventure on a 50/50 basis. We drove when it was our time whether it was city, mountains, night, snow, or ice. I fueled the truck if it was my turn for driving. I docked the truck if we arrived on my driving shift.

By our own preference, John generally took care of any truck issues, and I took care of paperwork issues, including dealing with brokers at border crossings. The chatter on the CB was not always very congenial towards women drivers, but you could turn it off.

In general, if I put on my company jacket and walked into the receiving area, I found that I was always well-received. At one particular site, the receiver asked John "Who is backing up your truck?" When John said it was his wife, the receiver came out and congratulated me.

Virginia Logan at the wheel; Nephew Jered in background.

Back to Back Driving

Virginia Logan

John hadn't been feeling great on our trip back from the West Coast. On our return to Grand Rapids, a visit to the doctor determined that he had 'a touch of pneumonia.' He needed to take antibiotics and rest, so we took some days out before our next load.

I drove first, making it much of the way to our drop-off at Grand Prairie, Texas. We picked up a load of oil out of Shreveport, Louisiana, and easily got back to Grand Rapids.

In the next several months, we drove three trips to Rocklin, California and two to Irvine. We carried bulk apples from Caldwell, Idaho to Kent City, Michigan; wood doors to Wichita, Kansas; dog food to Lewisburg, Ohio; and paper bags to Meijers in Lansing, Michigan.

Driving over the Donner Pass always brought to mind the story after which the pass was named: a party of westward-bound settlers was trapped in that area for four winter months, during which half of them died.

Donner ner- Lake

Donner is a mountain that truckers either love or hate. It's a mountain that demands respect, and I was finding that I actually loved the challenge of driving over it!

Over that first year, we also had several very long 'deadheads' (no-load-times). The first was a 1,096 mile dead-head from Boise, Idaho to Hastings, Nebraska to pick up animal hides going to Milwaukee, Wisconsin.

The second was after a 6-day layover in the Ontario, California 76 Truck Stop, including our first Thanksgiving away from home. We deadheaded 1,331 miles to Oklahoma City, Oklahoma to pick-up tiles going to Hardees in Fisher, Indiana.

That tile drop-off was our first experience of delivering a load to a construction site. No signs, no directions, no phones, lots of mud and no-one there knew anything!

After a Steelcase run to Clifton, New Jersey and back empty, we got a different truck. Our next run was with Haworth Furniture to San Francisco. This time, after unloading, we visited Fisherman's Wharf and ate seafood in a real restaurant.

The next day our dispatcher sent us to Medford, Oregon. A storm was headed into that area, so we wanted to get there, load and get out. I was driving up I-5 into Oregon. It is only about 30 miles from the border to Medford, but the State Port of Entry is about 15 miles into Oregon.

We had the required Oregon plate so all should have been fine. But as I slowed down for the entry ramp, I had trouble down-shifting this new-to-us truck, and then couldn't get it into gear after stopping on the scale. The weigh-master pounded on the truck window and said "Get this truck off my scale." I found a gear and moved it.

Our last run for December 1990 was carrying Shaw Walker furniture to Los Angeles, California. Because it was winter, we drove a southern route down I-44 thru Missouri and Oklahoma to I-40 and on across Texas, New Mexico and Arizona to Barstow, California.

As we discovered, I-40 averages about a 4,000-foot elevation from Texas thru Arizona and more than a 7,000-foot elevation at Flagstaff, Arizona. Despite being in the South, that elevation was just right for ice and snow.

Virgin River Gorge, AZ

Sure enough, John ran into the first ice in New Mexico. I started out at midnight, and after only three hours of driving, I'd had all I could stand. At one point, John stuck his head out of the sleeper and saw trucks on both sides of ours, and I was heading right up the middle between them. It was actually a couple of doubles stopped on both sides of the road to put on chains.

We averaged just 35 miles per hour all the way across Arizona. But that doesn't stop the trucking business. After our Los Angeles delivery, we were dispatched to pick up tires at DeLoera Tires in San Diego. It was Friday before the Christmas week-end.

We could not understand the gal from DeLoria Tires who was giving us directions to the pickup site. She seemed to be saying 'Coronado Street,' so when we saw an expressway sign saying 'Coronado,' we took the exit. Suddenly we were going over a long bridge to an island with a toll gate coming up.

If we paid the toll, we wouldn't be reimbursed. John zipped through the free bus gate, then turned around and rushed right on back across the bridge. We expected sirens, but got back free.

When we found DeLoera Tires, they were waiting and hand-loaded the tires. Off we went east to Laredo, Texas.

We encountered ice in San Antonio, and on all the bridges down I-35 to Laredo. We delivered the load of tires on Christmas Eve in Laredo, Texas and then headed to Houston for our reload of air-conditioning units going to Greenville, South Carolina and Greensboro, North Carolina. Then we deadheaded 104 miles to Lynchburg, Virginia, where we picked up printed material going to Allen Park, Michigan.

We were back home by the 30th of December and got to spend New Year's Eve at home.

An on-the-road Santa Claus salute

A Christmas Accident

John Logan

We saw road accidents on every trip we took across this country, thousands of them. I don't remember most, but some I can never put completely out of my mind. This story is about one of those times.

It was Christmas time. We had a loaded trailer of tires from San Diego, California going to Laredo, Texas. I was driving along on Interstate 8 and meeting road-ice in some places.

Along the Mexican border, we saw cars and pick-up trucks loaded with people, probably on their way to visit relatives for the holidays.

I was feeling kind of down because we had never been away from home and family for Christmas before this year. The only traffic on the road was an occasional big truck and lots of four-wheelers going home for the holidays. It was the middle of the night and plenty cold outside.

I was rolling along at a pretty good clip when I saw a light some distance up ahead. It was moving around and it soon became obvious that it was a flashlight. I jumped on the brakes and brought the truck to a stop next to the person holding the light.

I asked him if he needed any assistance and he said that he was just trying to get me to slow down. He shone his flashlight into the median. I was sorry he had.

There in the median among the bushes and cactus was a pick-up truck that had rolled over a number of times. It had a cap on the back of the truck and, of course, the cap went flying off as soon as the driver skidded on the ice and started to roll over. It was the saddest scene I'd ever seen: people had been thrown out of the back of the pick-up truck as it rolled over. They were lying, dead, all over the median.

The fellow who had stopped us had gathered the strewn packages into a pile and was throwing blankets over the dead people. I asked him if he needed to have the authorities notified. He said that they were on the way.

I had been feeling sorry for myself about being away from home at Christmas, but that seemed like a little problem in light of what I had just seen.

We listened closely to the radio all the way to Laredo, Texas in hope of getting some details about the accident. I heard nothing, but I was still saddened for these people who were not going to have a Christmas at all.

Texas Interstate

In and, Slowly, Out of Canada

Virginia Logan

We started January, 1991 with a load from Haworth Office Systems in Holland to San Antonio, Texas. We made it in plenty of time to sleep all night before we were unloaded in the morning. We were even able to go back to the Petro Truck Stop and have some lunch before we were dispatched.

This time it was a deadhead of 193 miles to Wadsworth, Texas. It was easy to head east on Interstate 10, cut off on Highway 71 to El Campo, then angle on over to Bay City. We found a safe shopping center lot to park in at about 10:30 p.m., went to bed and set the alarm for 7 a.m. That would give us time to go the last 10 miles and find OxyChem (short for Occidental Chemical Corporation) for a 10 a.m. loading time.

Quickly enough, 7 a.m. came. We looked out and saw we were closed in with a pea-soup fog! We were 20 miles from the Gulf Coast, so, despite the fog, we headed out to the OxyChem plant. We were told it was 10 miles from Bay City and the coast was 20 miles away, so we didn't think we could go too wrong.

We went through Wadsworth without seeing the plant, so we turned around, hoping we could spot something. This time we saw a sign and headed into the area—only to find ourselves in the middle of an array of 'danger' signs.

A fellow with a protective suit on was spraying something, but he motioned us ahead. Sure enough, there was a guard building, and we found that the way we had come in was definitely not the correct driveway.

The guards gave us instructions on what to do if the sirens went off. We also got helmets to wear if we were outside the truck. We were loading plastic resin going to Bramalea, Ontario, Canada. It is pretty scary to load up 45,000 pounds from a chemical plant, not knowing what you're exposed to.

So we headed back to Interstate 10 and turned east to Louisiana, north up through Mississippi, Tennessee, Arkansas and Missouri to Interstate 57 in Illinois.

At Effingham, Illinois we picked up Interstate 70 to Indianapolis, then up to Interstate 94 in Michigan. We headed to Detroit for the Windsor Bridge into Canada.

We had been told that all we needed to do was go to the Livingston Custom Broker with the paperwork and they would take care of everything. We had stopped for fuel at Dexter, Michigan and felt we were all set. It took about a half-hour at Customs; then we were on Route 401 in Ontario, Canada.

We caught some sleep at a service plaza and then found the delivery site in Bramalea. Once unloaded, we had a dispatch to reload at Canada Woodtape in Mississauga, Canada, just 14 miles away.

Wow! This was working out just great. We were loaded with edge binding for Westinghouse in Grand Rapids. We got out of the city and headed on Route 401 to Detroit. After stopping at a Service Plaza to eat, it was my turn for driving.

No one had explained to us that it was harder to get back into the USA than to cross from the USA into Canada.

We buzzed across the bridge to the U.S. Customs. The officer asked for our stamped manifest (a form that declares in detail what is being shipped across the border). We didn't have one.

He said we'd have to go back to the Canadian side and get a manifest from a broker, fill it out, get it stamped and return.

This was not only frustrating, but also expensive. We had to pay both bridge-tolls all over again, a cost that wouldn't be paid by the trucking company.

I made the turn around, went back to the Canadian side and found a broker who made out our manifest in triplicate, with a stamp. We headed back to the U.S. Customs. This time I handed the officer all my paperwork so that he could take what he needed and give back the rest.

Instead, he threw everything but the manifest away. I asked for my bill of lading and he said I hadn't given it to him. I said, "Yes I did," and he said "No, you didn't."

John said that we'd just sit there until he gave us back the bill of lading, but the Customs agent said "Oh, I don't think so. I'll call the Big Hook!" So we moved off to the side and John went inside to find out what could be done.

It turned out that all we could do was wait for the paperwork to be re-processed. The broker gave me a copy of the customs invoice and we made out a dummy bill based on that. We realized that we'd made a lot of mistakes. But crossing the border can be just as much hassle even when you know what you are doing and have everything right.

Ambassador
Bridge

Delivery in Washington, D.C.

John Logan

Have you ever driven a tractor-trailer unit 68 feet long during rush hour traffic in Washington, D.C.? If you haven't, hang on, because what follows will stretch your imagination.

Our truck was loaded with office furniture from the Westinghouse Company in Grand Rapids, Michigan, consigned to the Department of Veterans Affairs administration building, 810 Vermont Ave, N.W., in Washington, D.C. This is about two blocks north of the White House.

To start with, all truck traffic in Washington, D.C. is restricted to one route into and out of the city: Highway 50 (New York Avenue).

We were to be at 810 Vermont Ave., N.W. for delivery at 8 a.m. sharp. Normally, we plan city-site arrival early to beat the morning rush hour. So we arrived at 6:30 a.m. I got out of the truck and found the dock we had been instructed to use.

Everything seemed fine until I observed that the opening through the side of the building was 12 feet tall and the dock was at least 20 feet further inside the building. Our trailer is 13'6" high, making a problem.

I maneuvered the truck and trailer over until it was rubbing against the tree limbs along the sidewalk.

We sat and waited for the furniture installers to arrive at 8 a.m. Only then did we notice the sign saying "No Parking from 6 a.m. to 9 a.m." We decided not to leave.

As we waited, we watched the traffic volume grow. It reached an intensity that can only be described as bumper-to-bumper desperation. It also looked as if it might be against the law to crack a smile or look another person in the eye. 'Grim' was the look and mood.

The traffic didn't seem to have any problem getting around us. But at 7 a.m., a D.C. policeman showed up with his ticket book. When he began writing a ticket for our truck, I jumped down from the cab. I explained my problem and showed him my bills and instructions.

I also showed him the 12 foot doorway leading into the dock and my 13'6" trailer. I explained that I was 'up a creek without a paddle' until the government installers arrived and decided where they were going to unload the trailer.

This policeman did me a favor. He wrote a ticket for illegal parking, but then tore up his copy of the ticket. He instructed me to put my copy under the windshield wiper. He said that, with a ticket in place, no other cops would try to ticket my truck while I was waiting.

So we sat, waited and watched. Jinny even got out of the truck and started looking for Veteran's workers.

Then I noticed a different cop writing *another parking ticket*. I pointed at the ticket which I already had attached to the windshield. He simply climbed up on the truck and deposited a second ticket where the first one was attached. I blew my air-horn and tried to ask a question.

His answer was simply: "MOVE IT"! I said, "But the streets are totally jammed with cars and I have to deliver here."

He picked up his radio phone and called for the Big Hook to come and remove my truck. I decided that I had better do as I was told.

I looked at Jinny and said, "Two can play this game. If the cop wants to insist that I move this truck then I am going to MOVE THIS TRUCK."

I forced my way out into the bumper to bumper traffic and started driving around the block. As I came to the first corner, the traffic was backed up as far as I could see. To negotiate the corner took quite some time because our truck is very long and the corner was very tight.

It was a four lane street around all four sides of the Veterans building. I stayed in the middle of the lanes to make it impossible for anything but a bicycle to get around me while I moved along in granny-gear.

That made the people in the cars furious. They blew their horns and waved their arms wildly. Many flipped me the bird, which I took to mean that I must be number ONE in their book of wonderful and favorite people.

When I came to a corner, I moved the truck completely across the street blocking all four lanes. I had to make sure that I had plenty of clearance to make the corner and not hit anything.

This caused the people in the oncoming two lanes around the corner to back up, resulting in an entire block of traffic backed up, bumper to bumper. Car horns were blowing, but our truck was bigger. It got to be fun! I just waved my arms and yelled right back at the car drivers.

After I had made several slow-speed trips around the block at the magnificent speed of half a mile per hour, we did see the cop who gave me the ticket. He looked at me and shook his head! I blew my air horn and waved at him in a friendly way.

After a number of complete 'round the block excursions', the installers showed up. One fellow jumped up on the truck to find out what was going on and we told him the story. He said to just keep going in a circle until they could figure out where they would be unloading us.

Then we noticed that a lot of smokers were standing at the various entrances to the Veterans Building. They had noticed us and started to clap their hands and wave us on as we continued to circle the building. I kept moving at all times.

It took almost another hour before the installers came back with instructions.

We were to back the truck into the alley which goes through the heart of the building. After the time it took to miss all the cars now parked everywhere, we got our truck into the alley. The furniture had to be unloaded onto the ground and then carefully carried into the building to an elevator. This took several hours to accomplish.

It was a Washington, D.C. experience, for sure.

Our dispatch was a load in Virginia, west of Washington. So Jinny looked at the map and decided that we only had a short distance to the river, where we could catch I-66 into Virginia.

One-way streets were a problem in getting where we needed to go. A ring of very low railroad bridges surrounded the area, bridges dating back prior to the Civil War, when the vehicles were horse drawn stagecoaches.

We had quite a time getting through the traffic, but made it to the I-66 expressway headed to Virginia. Just as we started to cross the Potomac River, we saw a big sign that said, NO TRUCKS ALLOWED.

We were already going on the bridge, so we just put the hammer down and acted as if nothing was wrong. People looked at us and even a cop looked us over. We just kept going westbound.

I hope never again to be back in Washington, D.C. with a truck and trailer.

East Coast Blues

Virginia Logan

February of 1991 went along smoothly with a Herman Miller load to Rocklin, California, and a Slim Fast Beverages load back to Illinois. Then an Amway load of paper cartons out to Neutralite (an Amway subsidiary) in the Los Angeles area and back to Amway carrying cereal.

We drove two Westinghouse loads to the southern California area and picked up loads right back to Michigan. That made a nice average of 4,500 miles each week and a day at home in between each run.

That experience was a teaser for the week to follow. Or perhaps our dispatcher saw that we liked that kind of running. It's a special trucker's code: never tell the dispatchers what you really like or they'll give you the opposite for sure.

March began with a Westinghouse load of Office Furniture Systems out to Anaheim, California and a dispatch for a re-load from San Diego.

Off we went for the Convention Center in San Diego, arriving about noon Pacific Time. We found out that we were loading refrigeration units, used in a show that had just closed. They would be the last things out the door, and we were expected to be there and waiting whenever that moment happened to be.

That moment was not until 3 a.m. in the morning. Still, everything went well and we were on our way by 4:30.

Now we had to do our planning on Eastern Time because we were headed for the Convention Center in Boston, Massachusetts—3,400 miles east. The broker wanted us there by Friday, and no later than Saturday morning, just 72 hours away.

I knew that the best path for this time of year was through Arizona and New Mexico straight east to Dallas, Texas.

Arizona canyon road

Then we'd angle northeast, up through Arkansas and Missouri to Illinois. I-70 would take us across Indiana and Ohio to Pennsylvania, and Interstate 81 would join busy 84. On I-84, we could shoot right on across Connecticut and into Massachusetts, and then connect with the I-90 Turnpike that would take us straight into the heart of Boston!

All went well and we arrived at 5:30 am on Saturday morning. We were glad that it *was* a Saturday morning. The docking area was under the convention center with not much room for maneuvering a large truck. I had driven into Boston, but I decided that John would have the fun of that docking.

When our turn came around, John maneuvered and squeezed and pulled up several times, then got our trailer back to the dock without running over anything or damaging the truck. Our load came off quickly and easily and then we had to leave.

It was a weekend and our dispatch just said to hang out somewhere. 'Hang out' in Boston or close by with a big truck! That was going to be a challenge.

Our last encounter with a truck stop in Massachusetts had not been good. Our trusty directory indicated that if we went out to the outer beltway and headed south, there was a small truck stop at Wrentham.

First we had to find our way back to the main highway. Our inward directions had routed us in on 'one way' streets, so we had to find other streets to get back out. We found ourselves on a parkway that took us under a very large hospital. It was probably a 'no trucks' road, but heck, it was noon on Saturday. So we got out of the city in a hurry, headed south on I-495, and found a local truck stop.

This one was even worse than the last one we'd experienced. The parking lot was a dump, the restaurant was a greasy-spoon place and the showers were for men only!

If we went east, we'd be at Cape Cod. If we went south we'd be in Providence, Rhode Island which has one truck stop. If we had known what direction our dispatch would be on Monday, we could have gone back west to Sturbridge.

Instead, we stayed where we were. After scouting the area, we dropped our empty trailer in the lot and bobtailed to a little motel with a real restaurant that even had seafood. That saved the week-end.

When Monday morning came, we were showered and rested and ready to hit the road again. We got a dispatch for two pick-ups: Rockport Shoes in Leominster, Massachusetts; and Avanti Linens in Moonachie, New Jersey.

Our instructions were to arrive at 4 p.m. at Rockport Shoes. We hooked back up to our empty trailer and then went north to Worchester.

We arrived at Rockport Shoes at 4 p.m. and saw that everybody was leaving! We thought: "This sure is strange. Maybe it's just a shift change."

It wasn't a shift change. Everyone *was* leaving. I asked the shipping person which dock he wanted us at and who was going to load us up. He looked at me and said "There are the boxes. You load it". The boxes were lined up on the floor, six deep and about 50 ft across the warehouse. This was not going to be fun, a hand load-up from the floor with boxes that were not even on skids.

I asked the unfriendly shipping person if he had any 2 wheeled hand carts. He said there were some around someplace. I found them.

More than an hour later, with two of us hauling boxes with the hand carts, we had them stacked in the trailer.

We left that wonderful place and got out of Massachusetts. We figure it was only going to be about 250 miles (5 hours of driving) to New Jersey. When we got to Danbury, Connecticut, we put down for the night.

The instructions for the pick-up were to arrive at Avanti Linens at 10 a.m. Moonachie, New Jersey was just west of the George Washington Bridge and just south of Interstate 80. We had to come right down through the Bronx, paying tolls. The directions were to go through Little Ferry and turn left on Liberty Ave to Moonachie Road. Avanti Linens would be on the right side.

It was amazing that the directions were actually right. But, sure enough, it was a driver-load again. This time it was only 54 boxes, but they were huge and heavy. I could not even help pick them up, but the dock hand did help John.

Put together, we still didn't have a trailer full. But we were headed for Atlanta, Georgia, 818 miles away.

At 9 a.m. the next morning, we arrived. Our instructions were to go to the Gainey Trucking yard. We thought that would mean that we were dropping our trailer and heading out with something else and would not have to deal with unloading what we'd had to pile in.

That was half true. We did drop that load and deliver a Steelcase load to State Farm Insurance in Duluth, Georgia, just north of Atlanta. Then we returned to the Gainey Trucking yard to pick up that earlier load of shoes and linens for delivery to Ricks in Stone Mountain, Georgia the next morning. This would again be a driver-unload.

By the time we made it back to Michigan, we had gone 7,047 miles in two weeks.

Big Island, Virginia—
& John Loses His Grandmother

Virginia Logan

This story begins after a stop at the Manassas battlefield, off I-66 in Virginia. Our destination was a Georgia Pacific plant in Big Island, Virginia, where we'd pick up rolls of paper going to Milan, Michigan.

Our directions were: Take Highway 29 south to Lynchburg, Virginia, then Highway 501 north to Big Island. Supposedly, we couldn't miss the Georgia Pacific plant on that road. We didn't yet realize that a shipper never describes any problem getting to his location.

John made the exit onto Highway 29 South, a pretty good four-lane road. At Culpepper, Virginia, we switched drivers. This older road went through many little towns that we wished we could stop and explore. But we had to keep going to make Big Island and get loaded that evening.

We arrived at Lynchburg about 5:30 p.m., just as everyone in town was making their way out to Highway 501. When I headed north, at least a dozen cars were right on my bumper.

It was only about 25 miles from Lynchburg to Big Island, but suddenly the road began going into one switch-back turn after another. I didn't have any experience in this special kind of mountain driving. Mountains on an interstate are one thing and switch-back turns on a skinny two lane road are totally another. I had problems figuring out how much room I needed to negotiate these turns.

I thought I was managing, until I was on an inside curve and saw, coming around the bend heading towards me, another big truck.

John was yelling "Stay to the right, stay to the right" and I thought that I was doing just that. I saw the other truck start to run his trailer wheels into the guard rail, but I just kept going. We made it to the Georgia Pacific Yard, but I was a nervous wreck.

As we were getting loaded, I studied the map and discovered that we'd run into more switchbacks going up to Lexington where we'd catch I-64 to West Virginia.

John took it from Big Island. It was even worse in the dark, but he handled it.

We got the Georgia Pacific load delivered to Milan, Michigan, but when we returned to Grand Rapids we received a message that John's Grandmother, Carrie Bolen, had died in Cape Girardeau, Missouri. She had been a very special person to us and like a grandmother to our children in the years since John's mother had died.

We asked to take several days off to attend the funeral. We had stopped in Cape Girardeau not too long before this and knew that she was not doing well. We'd both had the feeling that we would not see her alive again.

This break in driving also gave us the opportunity to see our daughter Marie off to Paris. Marie had decided to quit her job at Hudson's and try life in Europe. I certainly could understand her desire for adventure, but the thought of not knowing when I might see her again was extremely difficult. So I was glad to have one last visit before she left.

It was a very emotional break from driving, but we appreciated the fact that we were able to be a part of these family events. One major problem with truck driving is that sometimes you just can't get to the place you need to be for your family in time.

John at Cape Girardeau cemetery

Breakdown in Rock Springs

John Logan

When we picked up a load of conveyor equipment from Rapistan Systems of Grand Rapids, Michigan, we were driving a new tractor-trailer. Our dispatcher had asked if we wanted to drive a fresh, new truck from Freightliner. Its engine was one of the newest, a Cummins N-14 with electronic controls.

Three manufacturers had been racing to market electronic engine controls. In the past, control was done by the 'governor' that limits idling and other speeds on diesel engines. This new computer controlled the speed and revolutions-per-minute (rpm) for every gear. It also regulated the fuel going to each cylinder and the horsepower output overall.

Presetting the computer allows the company to control how fast their truck can go, the amount of fuel it can use, and the amount of horsepower it can put out.

We were really enjoying the first run. Our new truck was powerful, moving down the road with very low rpm. More than 30 sensors told the computer what was happening at all times.

One of the amazing things about this motor was that it was set up for about 350 horsepower (hp). The only thing we had to do to make it a 550 hp motor was to tell it by computer that it was now a bigger motor.

Cummins wanted these engines on the road so badly that they offered a 500,000 mile warrantee on them.

We were moving along in Wyoming without any difficulty when I noticed that the fuel gauge was falling rapidly. I decided to stop and check the problem.

The next town was Rock Springs, Wyoming. I pulled the truck into a Nasty Knute's truck stop for a look-see. I had barely got the hood up when the problem almost hit me in the pant leg. A solid stream of fuel was shooting out the side of the fuel pump. The stream was a big as my little finger at about 40 pounds of pressure.

It doesn't take very long to pump a gallon of fuel out on the ground at that rate. Quite a few gallons had been pumped out before I realized that something was wrong.

We had a phone number for rapid response repairs which I called immediately. Then I called Gainey to tell them we were off the road. They called the 'big boys' at Cummins and a pump specialist came from the dealership right in Rock Springs.

As it turned out the N-14 prototypes had been built, tested and retested in the mines at Rock Springs. They had been run up to 1000 HP and tortured under the dirtiest conditions you can get, for five years. These people knew more about this new engine than anyone else in the entire United States.

It was Sunday afternoon by the time we got the truck into the garage. But what had happened turned out to be a very different problem. The pump assembly people had improperly installed an O-ring seal in the pump. And the Cummins dealer didn't have such a seal.

Because it was a new engine there were no spare pumps to be had closer than Salt Lake City, 200 miles away. It would take until mid-afternoon the next day to get them.

They pulled out tractor outside the building and told us they would see us in the morning. We weren't loaded with extra cash and so thought we'd just sleep in the truck for the night.

That night, the temperature dropped down into the single digits before midnight. We had blankets, but they were no match for those temperatures. We thought we might freeze to death before morning came. The motor could not be run so we had no heat!

We started out with one of us in the top bunk and the other in the bottom bunk. That didn't last very long when the cold started to settle into the truck. So we snuggled up close with the blankets and everything else we had along piled up on top. The whole inside of the truck turned to frost and so did we.

We sure were glad to see the people arrive that next morning for work. We went inside to warm up and get a cup of hot coffee. We fiddled around till afternoon, getting hungry since there was nothing to eat.

It was about 2 p.m. when the parts arrived from Salt Lake City. They turned out to be the wrong parts! That meant that we would have to wait another day for the proper parts to arrive.

We walked into town to get some food, but walking at 7,000 feet was a strange experience. I was huffing and dizzy all at once. It seemed like miles before we found a place to eat.

After that, I was happy for the meal, but unhappy about the prospect of sleeping in the truck that night. The temperature was going to go down to near the zero mark that night.

When we got back to the garage our mechanic asked me where we were going to stay that night. I told him "in the truck," just as we had the night before. He went straight to the boss, who apologized and offered to put us up in a motel for the night. We took him up on the offer without a moment's hesitation!

On Tuesday, the parts man arrived from Salt Lake City with an entirely new fuel pump. It took about 20 minutes to put it on the motor of our truck.

We jumped into that truck and turned the key. I'd never heard a sweeter sound than when that motor started to run. It even started to make some heat almost before we were hooked up to our trailer.

I don't think I will ever forget that feeling of desperate cold on that Sunday night in Rock Springs, Wyoming. After they had locked the gate and building, we were stuck like prisoners.

Never again would we let someone lock us up inside a fenced in area without a way to escape!

Wyoming roadway with snow

The Cockroach

John Logan

On our way from Dallas, Texas to Shreveport, Louisiana on Interstate 20, we noticed how rapidly the landscape was changing. East Texas is a very moist place with trees and bushes growing everywhere. The land here begins to roll in hills.

It had gotten dark and we were due for a shift change. I was hungry and knew that Jinny would be too when she woke up. So when I spotted a fairly large truck stop just short of the Louisiana border, I turned the truck into their parking lot.

The lot was full of drivers who had parked for the night. After several trips through the lot I spotted a place to put the truck. It was tight but with some wiggling, I got the truck safely parked.

We went inside and the place was cleaner looking than a lot of places we have stopped to eat. We found a booth situated just outside the kitchen. After we sat down, a waitress came over and gave us a menu. We ordered coffee and some sandwiches. As I remember, the food was pretty good.

While I was drinking a final cup of coffee, I looked in the direction of the kitchen and saw a cockroach. He was the biggest, fastest cockroach I'd ever seen.

He came straight out of the kitchen on a dead run for the booth where we were sitting, heading under our table to look for food. He didn't find any, so he made a beeline back to the kitchen again.

I sat there not believing what I had just seen. That cockroach had just come right out in front of everyone and gotten away with it.

I wasn't any too happy at the prospect that a cockroach might have run through my sandwich before I did, but it was a little too late to worry about it now. My sandwich was history.

When we went up to pay for our food, I told the cashier about the big, fast cockroach. She looked at me and said, "We do not have any bugs in this place."

I said, "But we just saw it go into the kitchen!"

She replied very quietly, "We told the boss. But he is too cheap to pay for extermination services and so we just look the other way."

We crossed that truck stop off our list of places to eat.

The Center of the 50 U.S. States
and a visit with Dad Logan

Virginia Logan

So far we'd had a lot of adventures and gained some depth of experience. What was going to be next?

A trip to Renton, Washington was a good start to the second half of 1991. We had never taken the northern route of Interstate 90 or 94, so off we went into the unknown.

It was June, so we had clear weather all across the country. We drove west from Grand Rapids to Council Bluffs, Iowa and headed north on Interstate 29. This route took us to Sioux City, Iowa, where three states come together and the Missouri River wanders south to Kansas City and then joins the great Mississippi River at St Louis, Missouri.

We drove through four hundred miles of rolling grasslands in South Dakota. At Rapid City, we stopped at the Windmill Truck Stop for some breakfast. It was early morning, but we had been able to see some of the Badlands National Park just before stopping. Then we drove past Sturgis, where the Harley Bikers gather every year.

Just north of Spearfish, South Dakota, almost to the state line, we saw a sign naming the 'Geographical Center of the 50 United States.' This designation was given in 1959, when Alaska and Hawaii became states. It is different from the 'center of the contiguous U.S.,' located near Lebanon, Kansas.

The nearby town of Belle Fourche claims attention as the place nearest to the spot in private pastureland marked by the U.S. Geological Survey.

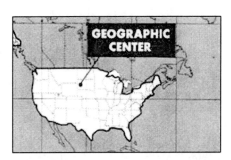

John & I were close enough to say that we drove through the center of the nation.

John then headed on across the state line into Wyoming, through Gillette and on towards the Bighorn Mountains and into Montana, 'Big Sky Country.'

We switched drivers at Lodge Grass in the Crow Indian Reservation, then I drove by the Little Bighorn Battlefield National Monument. The closer we got to Bozeman, the more mountains we saw. Crazy Peak is 11,214 feet high, Mt. Blackmore is 10,196 feet, Mt. Cowen reached 11,206 feet, and Hollowtop Mountain is 10,513 feet.

At Butte, Montana, the elevation climbs up along Deer Lodge and the Garnet Range in the Rocky Mountains. We stopped at Missoula's Crossroads Truck Center, had some dinner and 'put it down' for some sleep.

About 2 a.m., our trusty Kirk alarm rang and I got up. I went inside for the restroom and some fresh coffee. Then it was off west again.

One of the difficulties of getting up in the middle of the night to leave an area is figuring out how to get back to the freeway. We made sure to observe our way out before we went to sleep. If one of us was sleeping, the driver left a note with directions.

From Missoula it was only 100 miles to the Idaho state line and another 75 miles across Idaho. I thought that I would get well into the state of Washington in five hours, but it took me a good two hours to get to the Idaho state line at Lookout Pass. It must have been beautiful, but it was too dark to tell.

At Hayden, Idaho, a major construction project was underway, so traffic was rerouted through the town and out along Coeur d'Alene Lake. Detours are unsettling, especially in the dark.

I stopped to fuel at the Post Falls Flying J, just before the Washington state line. After another 60 miles into Washington, we stopped to switch drivers at Sprague. This stretch was easy-going across a desert area.

Since I wasn't driving, I could enjoy seeing Snoqualmie Pass, which was absolutely beautiful.

Snoqualmie Pass, Washington

We were headed for Superior Fast Freight at Renton, just a couple exits south on I-405. Five hours later the Shaw Walker furniture was unloaded. Our Gainey dispatcher said there was no re-load in sight, so we had to find a place to 'hang out' for the night.

On his earlier trip to Kent, Washington, John had visited with his father at Chehalis. So he knew there was a truck stop and restaurant at Napavine, just south of Chehalis on Interstate 5. We thought we might be able to connect with his dad again that evening or in the morning.

Off we headed to Napavine. We were starving by now, and so had dinner. John called his dad, who said he would come to the restaurant. We were glad of that because the prospect of taking the freightliner on a narrow, wet road and trying to park on soggy ground did not sound too smart.

John Sr. arrived after about an hour. He said that he had trouble finding his car, which he didn't use often and which had been hidden by grass grown tall. He had an oxygen tank on a little cart and said that his breathing wasn't good. We were shocked at his appearance, but we'd not given him any advance notice of our arrival.

In the restaurant, we found an out-of-the-way table where we could talk over some coffee. Talk we did, over coffee, then more coffee and pie, coffee and some more coffee for three hours.

When I excused myself for being tired, we all left the restaurant. The visit had been a good one because of all the talking, laughing, and remembering-when's that had taken place. But we were left with an uneasy feeling of something being wrong. In fact, it was the last time we would see him.

A Nevada Fine & Switchbacks
in California Mountains

Virginia Logan

The day after seeing John's Dad, we got a dispatch for a pick-up in Spokane, Washington. The pine molding from Spokane was heavy and it was going to Houston, Texas. We decided to try a different route south.

At Pocatello, Idaho, we took Highway 30 to Kemmerer, Wyoming and down to Interstate 80, then through Wyoming and Nebraska to Highway 81 south out of York. That took us down into Kansas where we caught I-135 and 35 at Wichita, right on down through Oklahoma City and to Dallas, Texas.

From there it was an easy shot over to Houston. Our return dispatch was a Goodman Electric load destined for both Ann Arbor and Southfield, Michigan. So we got home with a day off.

The next dispatch, Haworth furniture to Rocklin, California, was a familiar drive by now. We switched drivers at Lovelock, at about 11p.m. Eastern Time. It was very dark when I reached Sparks, Nevada, so I thought we might get through Nevada without the required, expensive fuel sticker.

Dark or not, Mr. Nevada Highway Patrolman saw that I did not have a state fueling decal on the truck. He pulled me over. When he asked for that permit and I couldn't produce the document, he asked for my driver's license, medical card, truck registration and logbook. After looking through it all, he did a 'walk around inspection' of the truck and trailer. He didn't get any 'extras' on me, but it cost $155.

He also said I could not proceed until I had gotten a fuel-permit. That permit cost $89.30. The permit cost was reimbursed by Gainey, but the company said it was our responsibility to get a trip-permit. We had to pay the $155 fine.

We still don't know how that patrolman could spot the absence of a decal in the dark.

Our next trip was another Rapistan Systems load of conveyors to Porterville, California. We went the southern route down through Missouri and Oklahoma City to Interstate 40, carefully avoiding Nevada. Our reload was a deadhead of 362 miles up to Red Bluff for paper egg cartons.

We stopped, fueled and got a bite to eat at the Petro in Corning. In the process, we ran into another Gainey driver named 'Doc'. He was going up to Red Bluff for a load of egg cartons also, so we continued on up to the Packaging Corporation together. John and I dropped our trailer and picked up a trailer already loaded for Knob Noster, Missouri.

Doc knew a shortcut. He said that Highway 36 went straight east out of Red Bluff over Lassen and into Susanville. From there it was just a short way down 395 to Reno. He mentioned a few 'tight turns', but said they weren't a problem.

John liked the challenge of a new route, and, since he would be driving, I figured those tight turns would be his problem and not mine.

Doc's idea was to head down Highway 89 which would bring us into I-80. So off we went headed into the Lassen National Forest. Pretty soon we came to a sign saying, 'Tractor-Semis over 30 feet Kingpin to rear axle not advised next 8 miles.' I was glad that John was driving and that traffic would be scarce.

Up and down, zig and zag around those 15 mph curves. Little 'black tail' deer, about the size of a large dog, were grazing by the road everywhere. The bucks had antlers the size of a bigger deer. They kept eating and paid no attention to us going by.

More curves. Up and down hills we went, as John and I both got more tired. We made it to Verdi, Nevada and got the fuel permit.

That night, I thought I'd never drive those curves and switch-backs again. About a year later, I drove through those same 8 miles without a problem. Experience makes a lot of difference.

Black-tailed Deer

OUR FIRST RIDER

Virginia Logan

The cab of a truck is mighty small with two people trying to live in it. Two sets of clothes are hanging in the closets, along with shoes, personal effects, and bags for carrying your things into truck-stop showers. There are books, maps, company information like payroll envelopes, office supplies, and a portable TV.

Yet we both wanted to have our family know what this trucking was like. When our son Jason agreed to come along for a trip, we were thrilled.

We had gotten home from the previous round on Friday afternoon and had to leave again for a Rocklin, California load on Saturday. The delivery time was 7 p.m. Pacific Time on Monday, so we had plenty of time. We got to the Gainey terminal about 3:30 p.m. Saturday and bobtailed to Zeeland to pick up the trailer for Rocklin. After hooking up, we drove over to fuel at the Tulip City Truck Stop.

We hadn't eaten before we left, so we decided to treat Jason to a truck stop dinner at a Petro 2 stop in Benton Harbor, Michigan.

Then it was time to figure out sleeping arrangements. Of the two bunk beds in a truck, the lower one is larger and more comfortable. The top one is adequate, but not great to use on a rough road. We put straps on it so Jason would feel secure, but he soon decided that the straps weren't really necessary, at least in the flatlands.

Out we headed across Illinois with John driving. Then I drove five hours on into Iowa and through Des Moines, which had a Sunday morning quiet. I was ready to switch at 6:30 a.m., and pulled off on a ramp that said 'Dexter.'

The next thing that I knew, John was stopping at Odessa, Nebraska. We were at the 'Big Red Coffee Pot in the Sky'. This restaurant has a truckers area equipped with a large television screen playing nonstop films. We ate lunch and browsed through the trucker's store before heading on into Wyoming.

Everyone was awake when we reached the top of Sherman Hill, so we stopped for pictures.

Jason
& John
at top of
Sherman Hill;
Lincoln
statue
to right
of truck

I was driving again in the early morning hours of Monday morning: over the Sisters on the western end of Wyoming, into Utah and the Wasatch Range. This was a favorite stretch of highway that I'd have liked Jason to see, but he was sound asleep.

On over Parley Summit and the ski areas, through Salt Lake City and across the Salt Flats. John drove across most of Nevada while I slept.

After a driver-switch, I drove to the Boomtown Casino and its super-buffet. Jason really enjoyed the buffet and chose 3 pieces of our favorite dessert, cheesecake!

We called the dispatch office and found out that after our Rocklin delivery, we'd be heading up to Red Bluff for another load of egg cartons. It was August, we were doing just great on time, and the weather was beautiful.

So we stopped at the Gold Run Rest Area. John had read that gold mining was done here in the early settlement days and the stop had historical displays showing how the mining was done.

We wandered the trails, hoping to spot a shiny piece of gold. It was wishful thinking.

Jason & John on the trail of gold

Then we were on to Rocklin, where we dropped the trailer and picked up an empty. Since we had our destination, we could head north to Red Bluff for the egg cartons.

Jason did see the Bonneville Speedway out on the salt flats, where they were racing at this time of year. He also saw the Tree of Utah (picture on right) on the Salt Flats. This memorial was made by the Swedish artist Karl Momen for his daughter, who was killed in an accident there.

On through Salt Lake City, with a stop at Echo, Utah. We saw wild horses in the canyons and we ate at the Echo Café, which has the best Scandinavian scones. Then we settled in for the long night's ride back East, through Nebraska, Iowa and into Minnesota.

We arrived at Crystal Foods at 8 a.m. to deliver the egg cartons and discovered that we were expected to unload them. These cartons are packaged in bundles that weigh only about 25-30 pounds, but they are loaded from the floor to the trailer's ceiling. Jason with his 6 foot, 2 inch height and long arms was very welcome in those 2 1/2 hours of work.

John called dispatch to let them know that we were ready for a load. Instead of bringing us back to Grand Rapids, we were told to load up at Barrel O'Fun in Perham, Minnesota and head west for Santa Ana, California.

That meant we had to find different transportation back home for Jason. A few calls told us that a 'spur of the moment' flight for Jason from Minneapolis to Grand Rapids had a steep price. Amtrak had a much better deal with a ticket for $107. Jason told us later that he enjoyed the train ride and got to Grand Rapids about 10 p.m. the same night.

Wyoming
Route 487

To California via Medicine Bow

Virginia Logan

After dropping Jason at the St. Paul Amtrak Station, John and I had three whole days to get to southern California. Gainey paid us the miles that a computer showed as the distance, not the actual miles driven. They wanted drivers to come within a 10% range of those miles, but didn't care what route you chose.

We decided to head west on Interstate 90 and then turn south in Wyoming on I-25 to I-80. When we got to Gillette, Wyoming, we stayed the night and then planned to add a little shortcut to our trip.

John had taken a hunting trip out to Wyoming a few years back to hunt antelope. The trip had been quite an experience for him and the little shortcut would take us right through the area.

At Casper we headed off along the Shirley Basin on route 487. At one point we came across a sign that said 'Rough Road Ahead.' To be correct it should have said 'No Road Ahead.' It was totally under construction.

When there was a road, it was like a ribbon stretching as far as the eye could see. Antelope were grazing right along the fence by the road. This area is one of the most windswept on the North American continent and has one of the first electricity-generating windmills.

We came to Medicine Bow, named because Indians came to the area for the trees (nonexistent now) from which they made their bows. The word 'medicine' meant good. 'Good bows' was the translation.

The Virginian Hotel is also at Medicine Bow. It is a restored old time frontier hotel in the National Register of Famous Places, where the television series 'The Virginian' was shot. The hotel bar is 'L' shaped and made from a huge tree split right down the middle.

The rooms upstairs are just as they were in frontier days with a community bathroom at the end of the hall. The walls in the dining room held pictures of when hundreds of deer, elk and antelope would come right into town during the winter months for food.

The Virginian Hotel at Medicine Bow

Yes, we had to have a meal here and speculate about what it was like in the days when this place was built. Then we continued on our way south.

A Scenic Shortcut

Virginia Logan

This story starts as we drove our usual path from Rocklin, California, north to Red Bluff for egg cartons. They were loaded and we were ready to leave at 3:30 p.m. Finally, we had an opportunity to try a daytime shortcut over Lassen Peak, through the Lassen National Forest and over to Susanville, the county 'seat.' From there, the highway runs straight down to Reno, Nevada.

It was a beautiful day and I was happy to do the camera work and leave the driving to John.

We headed eastbound through fields strewn with lava rocks, then up into the 15 mph, 35 mph and 40 mph curves. The higher we went the larger the trees were until we hit Morgan Summit at 5,750 Feet elevation. As we descended, the trees along the roadway were so straight and tall that it felt like we were passing through a very high archway.

We drove through the little town of Chester and by Lake Almanor (called 'the point where the Sierras meet the Cascades'). As we were climbing out of the valley, John pulled over on the shoulder. He said that I had to get a picture of what he was seeing in his rearview mirror! So I jumped out, walked out in front of the truck, and turned around to see what he was so excited about.

There was Mt. Lassen on the horizon just as clear as could be. I aimed and snapped a picture and it was the last one! That was before cameras went digital and a film allowed taking only a limited number of pictures. The photo turned out so well that we enlarged it to hang in our home.

Mount Lassen in center background

Our route took us over Freedonyer Pass at 5,748 ft. elevation before it dropped into Susanville at 4,200 ft. elevation. From there we joined Route 395 and ran along the east side of the Sierra Nevada Range down into Reno. Lots to see, but the highlight was Mount Lassen.

Daughter Marie Rides Along

Virginia Logan

Several east-to-west trips later, we had three days at home, just as our daughter Marie was flying in from Europe to Detroit Metro. Marie didn't know that we, not a friend of hers, would be waiting for her arrival.

Since it was an international flight, the passengers went to customs first and one by one were coming out into the lobby, but we didn't see Marie. We found out later that Customs had detained her because of her extended stay and travels.

She might have been 'a suspicious character' in their minds, but we were glad to see her come through the door. *She* was so surprised to see *us* standing there!

Marie came back to Rockford with us. On the following day, we received a dispatch for a Rocklin, California load, and Marie decided to come along. We were surprised and delighted. That meant we would get all the details of her last five months of travel.

Off we went on a nearly non-stop drive to California. We did stop at the Wendover Casino to try our luck, so it was the next morning when we headed over to Rocklin.

John & Marie on desert road

Our dispatch from Rocklin was more egg cartons, going to Edwards, Mississippi. We headed on south on Interstate 5. We did stop at the Petro in Corning to fuel, eat, and shower. Since we had over three days to get to Mississippi, we stayed for the night.

At this particular Petro, we had several times seen a man who always wore a full set of leather chaps, boots with spurs, and a leather vest. We had wondered if he was a local character or, like us, a truck driver. This time, John struck up a conversation and found out that he was indeed a truck driver, but was about to give it up. He just liked to wear the leather outfit.

On the road, you can pretend lots of things. Some guys dress like a cowboy, or a 'high plains drifter' with the black cowboy hat and long duster and boots. There are always 'California' drivers with shorts and sandals no matter what the weather. Out of the truck, John and I were often mistaken for retired tourists.

We headed on south to Bakersfield, across Route 58 and the Tehachapi's to Mojave, then south on Route 14 to Lancaster. It was Friday and we had extra time, so we had called John's brother Charles to see if we could stop for a visit. They were delighted to be able to also visit with Marie and hear her stories.

Charles brought us back to our truck and John continued driving on down through Los Angeles and out Interstate 10 to Blythe, on the border between California and Arizona. It was about 5 a.m. Pacific Time when I started my shift of driving. Soon the sun started to come up. That can be a very difficult time of the morning to drive, but I never minded if I was just starting.

Marie joined me in the front seat. We talked and enjoyed the beautiful morning. The horizon was hazy, but there was nothing blocking the sun on this straight and flat stretch of roadway.

In the distance ahead, I was aware of two trucks. One had been passing in the left lane when suddenly I saw a lot of dust or smoke. I'd turned the CB off, so I wasn't aware of a problem ahead. My first thought was that one truck had blown a tire.

Then I realized that they were braking hard, so I started braking also. By the time I came to a stop, the trucks ahead of me were inching along slowly through what looked like personal stuff strewn all across the road.

In the left lane was an Arizona Patrol car, its lights flashing, that had been smashed along one side. As I pulled up along the patrol car, a policeman stopped me, so I asked what had happened. All he could say was "I got this car new yesterday and now look at it. Just keep moving."

I kept driving through the mess while trying to figure out what had happened. Finally I realized that there had been an accident in which a four wheeler hauling a trailer loaded with belongings had lost control and dumped its load all across the highway.

At the point when the patrol car blocked the left lane, two freight trucks were coming, one passing the other in the left lane. Blinded by the rising sun, the driver didn't see the patrol car. He had probably slammed on his brakes and maneuvered to miss the car, but his trailer obviously didn't.

I was just glad it wasn't us driving in that left-hand lane! We continued on across the hot southern desert.

One of many interesting
signs along the road

In New Mexico, we stopped at a rest area west of Las Cruces and took some pictures by the tall bamboo growing there (on right). Marie said the scenery looked like the Turkish countryside where she'd traveled.

On through El Paso, Texas and, over 800 miles later, we were in Shreveport, Louisiana. It was Sunday night and we couldn't deliver this load until Monday, so we just went to the east side of Louisiana and spent the night at the Tallulah Truck Stop.

The next morning we found Cal Maine Foods at Edwards, Mississippi in spite of the sketchy directions. We delivered the egg cartons, and our dispatch said to pick up a load of furniture at Columbus, Mississippi. That was only 150 miles away, and the pickup was the next morning.

We decided to splurge and get a motel for the night in Columbus. Cruising through Columbus, we didn't spot any motel at which we could park the truck. But we had spotted a small mall area with some restaurants close by, and even a movie theater. So we had dinner and went to a humorous version of a Robin Hood movie.

In the morning we got our load of Tombigbee Furniture to be delivered in Livonia, Michigan. We would be going right by Ann Arbor and could drop Marie off. She had traveled nine days with us, caught up on her sleep, and was ready to tackle life back in Michigan. We had enjoyed hearing all the stories and just having her traveling with us.

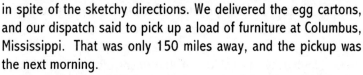

Raw Hides & Barn Cats

Virginia Logan

After our trip with Marie, we got on the road from Grand Rapids to Colorado Springs. Then we deadheaded 358 miles to Iowa Beef Packers (IBP, then the world's largest meat processor) in Lexington, Nebraska. We were to pick up a load of 'flat critters' (hides) from IBP that were headed to Michigan Office Furniture in Grand Rapids, Michigan.

We all know that producing the meat that we eat requires killing cattle. But to see the animals getting off the cattle trucks, herded into pens on one end of the plant—and know that you are picking up the hides at the other end of the plant was almost too realistic.

IBP information told us that the plant processes 200 cattle an hour and about 1600 every shift.

We were glad to leave this place.

Our first October run covered 7,008 miles. We started in Grand Rapids with a Westinghouse Office Furniture load that had three delivery points. The first was at Ogden, Utah; the second in San Jose, and the third in Campbell, California. From there we took wood doors from Rocklin, California to Star Lumber in Wichita, Kansas; then pet food to the Gainey yard in Atlanta, Georgia.

In Atlanta we picked up a loaded trailer of refrigeration units going to Lewisville, Texas. After a 'deadhead' of 258 miles to James River in Fort Smith, Arkansas, we got a load headed to Battle Creek, Michigan.

From Battle Creek we headed right back out with a Haworth load to Philadelphia, Pennsylvania, and then back to Michigan.

We had three days off, but not off the road. My youngest sister, Rosie, was getting married, so we drove to Indianapolis, Indiana. She didn't expect us, and was delighted. It was great to be together for a happy occasion.

We followed that good time with a rush Shaw Walker load going to Newport News, Virginia. The building we delivered to was scheduled for a grand opening and someone had goofed on getting the final load of office furniture delivered. It was only 800 miles, but we were pressured to get there on time.

Our reload was to go to the Sewell Port Docks in Norfolk, Virginia. We picked up raw rubber from Indonesia, headed to Corduroy Rubber in Grand Rapids, Michigan. That weird, jello-like load would be turned into hoses, floormats, transmission belts and gaskets.

Our last October run had a peculiar twist. It was another load for Rocklin, but when we reached Verdi, the road over Donner Pass was closed by a snow storm. At the truck stop, we met another couple who were also delivering at Rocklin in the early morning. They had decided to try the Feather River route.

This route heads north out of Reno on Highway 395 and then west on Route 70. It is 105 miles from Verdi to Rocklin over Donner, but the elevation is 7,000 feet. Route 70 is 200 miles, but goes up just to 5,200 feet.

Since the snow level was supposed to be above 5,000 feet, the longer-but-lower path seemed like a good alternative route. It was raining and other truckers were also choosing the Feather River route.

We got over Beckwourth Pass at 5,221 ft. and the roads were still good. After a number of little towns, we reached Lee Summit at 4439 ft. Then our road ran along the Feather River, where road conditions started to change.

The road got narrower, with more curves and narrow tunnels in which we had to straddle lanes to get through. There was a narrow, very long bridge over Feather River. Then came a sign saying: 'Truck route ENDS'!

No one had mentioned this problem. We were already over halfway on this route so, along with other trucks, we kept on going. It was miserable and long, but we made it to Rocklin.

The long bridge over the Feather River

On Thanksgiving Day we were in Red Bluff, California, with our trailer loaded for Loda, Illinois. It was a day with beautiful sunshine, so we decided to take the shortcut over Lassen. This time, I was driving. It was our fifth time on that route, and I had been watching just how John drove it. It *was* a challenge, but thrilling to accomplish.

An interesting delivery took us to Oshkosh, and then Beloit, Wisconsin. Our delivery directions ended with looking for a mailbox that would say 'R.J. Skinner.'

We found our way, but almost missed the mailbox that said 'R.J. Skinner,' since it was just a farm house and barn. I told John that I'd go up to the house, knock and ask for Skinner. A fellow came out and said "Yup, that's me. I'm having lunch and when I finish I'll be right out. Just come on down the driveway."

There was barely room to turn into the driveway, but John did an excellent job and we waited for R.J. Skinner to finish his lunch and come back out. He set up a couple of planks from a cement slab to our trailer and we unloaded.

Several barn cats came out to watch the proceedings. They'd run and hide, but their curiosity was always too much and they would come back. This was the most unusual unloading situation of our trucking life.

That year, we spent Easter with John's brother and family in Las Vegas, Nevada; the 4th of July in Flint waiting to deliver to a grocery warehouse; Thanksgiving on the road over Lassen in California; Christmas at home and New Years in Georgia.

Our Almost-Load

Virginia Logan

1992 started off innocently enough with a short run to Topeka, Kansas. We were rested up after spending some time at home over the New Year. So, on our return from Kansas, we turned right around with a load of Westinghouse Office systems to South San Francisco, California.

No reloads were available, so we headed across the Bay Bridge to the closest truck stop, at Fairfield. There was a Jason's Restaurant, or we could walk across the overpass to some fast food spots on the other side of the expressway. It wasn't fancy or particularly clean, but Jason's had the necessities: bathroom, phones and food.

The Two-level San Francisco Bay Bridge

On the third day, we got a dispatch to go to Norvell Company in San Jose for a load. That was about an hour and a half away, and it felt good to be moving again. We arrived about 10 a.m. Pacific time. The company started loading up our trailer.

John always likes to see just what is going into the trailer, even if we are not required to keep count. What he saw were computer components, so, out of curiosity, he asked the value. He was told that the first half of the trailer would probably be about $1.25 million and the second half of the load would be a total of about $1.5 million.

That's not only a lot of dollars worth of responsibility, but he wondered if Gainey Trucking had enough insurance to cover that liability. So he asked if I knew about the insurance.

I found the answer in the book holding the permits. Gainey's insurance coverage was only $125,000 per trailer. That limited coverage made this load a big potential problem.

John got on the phone to our dispatcher and explained the situation. Mark, our dispatcher, said, "Stop everything right now. Don't let them put anything more on the trailer until we discuss this."

As you might guess, Gainey had no idea of the high value of that load. We'll never know whether it was an oversight on someone's part, or whether someone purposefully undervalued the contents to keep shipping costs low. In either case, we were fortunate that we discovered the problem and hadn't ended up hauling a $2.75 million load with only $125,000 in insurance.

Egg Cartons & Boxes of Plastic

Virginia Logan

After the lost load of computer items, we were reassigned to Packaging Corporation of California at Red Bluff, where we'd get a load of paper egg cartons the next day. That was 215 miles north, but we were glad for the change of scenery. We also knew that there was a big truck stop at Corning.

The egg cartons were consigned to Southern New England Egg Farms at Under the Mountain Road, Franklin, Connecticut. So we were going to drive over 3,000 miles in 3 days, straight across the U.S.

I started driving, heading straight down Interstate 5 to Sacramento. From Interstate 80 it was eastbound all the way: Nevada, Utah, Wyoming, Nebraska, Iowa, Illinois, Indiana toll road, Ohio turnpike, Pennsylvania and New Jersey, straight across the George Washington Bridge past New York City. North on Interstate 95 along the shoreline of Long Island Sound into Connecticut. Then Interstate 95 to the east of the state and north up I-395 to Norwich.

Our delivery directions were: Go north on Highway 32 out of Norwich, past the John Deere Dealer about 1/4 mile, turn right on Plains Road, go 1/2 mile and take the left fork, go about 1/4 mile and you'll see the sign on the left.

After 58 hours of driving, those were scary directions, but we actually found the Southern New England Egg Farm at 9:30 p.m., exactly 3 days from when we left Red Bluff, California.

We already had a dispatch for the next morning at the Frem Corporation in Massachusetts. After we unloaded, I headed back to Norwich, then north on I-395, which went straight up into Massachusetts. Just past the I-90 turnpike was Worcester.

It was 2 a.m. and raining. We didn't have directions to the Frem Corporation and didn't spot any truck stops.

So John got on the CB and started asking for local information. Pretty soon a fellow came on asking what we needed. He seemed to know about the Frem Corporation, but we were already past the exit. We went to the next exit and headed back south again.

It is hard enough to understand people on the CB and this fellow with the local information had an accent that was frustrating for us mid-westerners. But he did guide us to the Frem Corporation, so we were ready and waiting for our load at 7 a.m. that morning.

We had been able to get only a few hours of sleep before our load time, and then got the news that the load of boxes of plastic items had to be hand-loaded. We recorded 3 1/4 hours for each of us 'on duty' to hand-load this trailer.

John loading boxes

We were really beat now and our handy directory of truck stops indicated that there was a fairly large stop at Sturbridge just about 30 miles east of where we were.

We took a highway parallel to the turnpike which should have taken us right past this truck stop. We missed it and had to turn around and backtrack. We went right by it again before we realized that a parking lot with trucks crammed in was the truck stop.

We ate, and then John drove east on Interstate 84, taking us back across Connecticut.

That evening on our way across Connecticut, we were listening to the radio as we went through Hartford. That's how we heard that the U.S. had attacked the Iraqis in Kuwait.

We had our portable TV with us, but we couldn't get any channels. So it was not until we returned home that we saw actual footage of the attacks.

The Philadelphia Squeeze

John Logan

Driving a truck into a very old city, built when a horse with a buggy was the normal transportation, is an experience not to forget. Streets are narrow and the corners are crowded with signs. Even a small truck pulling a small trailer has a hard time driving in these cities. For an 18-wheeler, they are a nightmare.

We were loaded with Haworth Office Furniture going to Mid-Atlantic Installers at 25th St. and McKeen, not far from the center of Philadelphia, Pennsylvania.

Our directions looked simple.

"Take I-76 to exit 43 B -Passyunk Ave.
At the first light turn left and go 4 blocks.
Mid-Atlantic is on the corner of 25th & McKeen.
Use caution entering driveway under the concrete
overpass; tops of the support columns are
larger than the middle."

I missed the turn at 25th. Then I glimpsed a street that seemed to go right to our destination. As I started down this street, it began to close in on my truck. Tree limbs were hanging down and cars were parked on both sides of the already-narrow street. When I got to the corner where I thought I'd turn right onto 25th St., I discovered that cars were parked right up to the corner itself.

That left no room to swing the truck around to go right. I wiggled the truck around and got as close to the left side of the street as I could without damaging a parked car. Then I tried turning again. When the trailer was about halfway around the corner, I saw it was making contact with a stoplight that had been put right on the corner curb.

I only needed another 5 inches, so in desperation, I decided to snuggle the trailer up against the light and try making the light turn around on its post as I slipped around the corner.

The extreme angle of the trailer and the tree limbs meant I couldn't see very well. I asked Jinny to take the wheel while I spotted from the outside, giving her directions as to which way to turn and when to pull forward.

I was just getting the stop light to turn on top of the post when a Philadelphia policeman arrived. He showed me his badge and said he was tired of truckers tearing down city signs.

I said, "Just a moment. I haven't torn down any signs." He said, "Well, what do you call that little project you got going now?" I said that I was only trying to get the light to turn on the top of the post where it was sitting. He said, "I should take you down town and put you in the hoosegow."

I got back in the truck and backed it off the stop light very carefully. But I knew that if I backed all the way around the corner, I would smash some parked cars.

In desperation, I looked across the street and noticed that it looked as if I could drive under the elevated expressway and get myself turned around. I pulled the truck ahead and sure enough I was able to get the truck under the expressway. It looked as if I could go all the way down to the delivery address.

About three blocks down, I discovered that the space was getting too low for my trailer. I tried to pull the truck out between the large support columns and make a left turn onto 25th Avenue.

That was when I thought back to the message in our directions about the width at the top of the support columns.

Every time I tried to get out, I would hit the top of the trailer. The base of the cement columns flared out, so I got another idea. I would run the drive wheels over that flared-out base, and that would make the truck tip away from the column just enough so that the top wouldn't hit up above.

My tactic worked, so the tractor and half the trailer were out on 25th Avenue. But the street was so narrow that if I turned the tractor to go down the street, I would tear the trailer wide open.

I felt desperate! Then I saw a driveway going into someone's garage. I turned the tractor up that driveway until the nose of my tractor was almost hitting his garage. I still couldn't back up because the trailer would hit the cement column behind my truck.

My choices were down to one. I hooked the tractor into low gear, made a left turn and drove across someone's green space. Unloading looked easy now, compared to the effort of getting the load to the delivery spot.

The Nevada Drunk

John Logan

We were westbound in Nevada on Interstate 80. It was one of those nights when everything is going smoothly, so smoothly that it gets downright boring. The weather was good and the wind was calm. I had gone through Winnemucka, Nevada and, as I rolled along I encountered a flatbed truck loaded with lumber.

Soon that driver and I began a game of *swap places*. I would pass the load of lumber, and then he would get tired of following and would pass me. We rolled westerly-bound past Puckerbrush, Nevada.

A small size Toyota pick-up truck joined our lineup and we had a convoy going. It didn't take long before he was switching places in line right along with us.

We were about twenty miles west of Puckerbrush and approaching Rye Patch Dam when an old Chevrolet pick-up of early 50's vintage came screaming out of the median. He darted to the right shoulder, passed all three trucks and cleared the lumber truck that was leading the parade.

At this point, the Chevy driver cut right in front of the lumber truck and slammed on his brakes. The driver was alert and managed to avoid hitting the old Chevy.

We were just about to top over a hill as we approached Rye Patch Dam. The Chevy had stomped on its gas pedal and disappeared over the top of the hill.

Then a crazy thing happened. I saw the lumber truck's brake lights come on as he swerved to the right shoulder. I put my rig on the shoulder as well because by then I could see something was in the middle of the road. The Toyota pick-up was in the left lane.

Both of the big truck drivers were sitting up high and, as a result, could see that there was something blocking the road. I stopped on the shoulder of the road right next to the block—which was the Chevy, parked in the middle of the road, cross-ways with lights out!

The fellow in the Toyota pickup didn't have a chance. He hit the old Chevy square in the middle of the driver's side. Fortunately for him, the Chevy driver was standing in the median, just watching the chain of events. But the Toyota driver was battered and bruised, with a couple cuts from flying glass. He got out of his truck and walked to the side of the road.

I grabbed some flares and started back on the road to stop approaching traffic. Along with the flares, I started waving a flashlight.

Trucks were coming fast. When they saw me, their tires screamed as they braked. The first truck topping the hill saw the wreckage in the middle of the road and went to the left because the right shoulder was blocked by our trucks. There was a deep ditch on that edge of the roadway, so I don't know how he held it, but he did get around the wreckage.

Jinny was on the CB in our truck, talking to the drivers as they approached our location. She hoped that she could get them slowed down before they got to where I was flagging them down.

Suddenly I heard the air horn blowing on my truck. I looked around and the crazy Chevy driver was trying to get into the truck with Jinny. She had locked the door and was blowing the air horn for all she was worth.

I ran toward the truck. The other two truck drivers also came running from the brush where they had been looking for what we'd concluded was a drunk. When the drunk decided that he'd make for the bushes, the lumber-truck driver and Toyota driver went in hot pursuit.

After our truck was nearly hit several times, I moved it clear of the accident scene. Meanwhile, the other fellows caught the drunk and had him down on the ground. There was a lot of kicking and punching going on.

At this point, I noticed flashing lights and heard the siren of an approaching police car. The other two drivers came up with the drunk in tow. They had both his arms twisted up behind his back somewhere in the vicinity of his ears.

The cop took the drunk and said he would put his butt in the cruiser. But first, he asked why the drunk was so beat up. We had only gotten a few words out when the drunk bolted, running for all he was worth.

Grabbing his two foot long maglite, the cop ran after the drunk, who had run face first into a four-strand barbed wire cow fence. That wire had long tines to effectively keep cattle that have a mind to wander in place. After hitting the cow wire at full speed, the guy managed to squeeze through the fence wire and keep going.

The cop got tangled in the top wire, then started out after the drunk again, and shortly had him on the ground.

After a couple of good whacks, he got handcuffs on the man and they started back toward the cruiser. Then, when they got back to the fence, the cop grabbed him by the scruff of the neck and belt and rubbed him against the fence wire before pushing him over.

When a back-up unit arrived, the cop told them he wanted to personally take this drunk into the hospital for drug and alcohol tests. He then pointed to his crotch and you could see that he was going to need some medical help himself.

Each of us filled out a report about the incident and went on our way. An ordinary trip had turned into an incident that made a good story.

Virginia's father, Van; Marie, John and Jason at Eaton School graduation

Truck stop at Excalibur Casino Las Vegas. Nevada

Tunnel through Freedonyer Peak, California

Marie & Jason by our truck

John, Charles & David Logan,
Thanksgiving Day, outside
David's home

Virginia with
Nephew
Kevin

Almost Scammed

John Logan

We arrived near New Orleans on a Friday morning that was unusually cold. Like most large American cities, New Orleans has only one truck stop. When we got our load off, we called our dispatcher and were told to find a place to hang out and call back later in the day.

We decided to go north of the city and wait in a Petro Truck Stop about 30 miles away. As the day wore on we called dispatch a number of times with no success. Finally, at the end of the day we were told that we would just have to hang out for the weekend because they had no loads available until the following Monday morning.

The one truck stop inside of the city is called the Mardi Gras stop. We got directions into the area and started south over the longest bridge we'd ever seen, over the swamp which is itself north of Lake Charles.

We arrived and got the last available truck parking place. The area and the people both looked very rough. We were discussing our options when we were approached by a fellow who had just driven into the parking lot from the street

He said "Psssssst! Hey bud, are you interested in a video-tape machine for your truck?" I said I had a TV but that I had no VCR. He said, "Come over here then," and backed his car between two trailers. He kept telling me to be discreet and keep my voice down.

He reached into a sack he had on the front seat and pulled out a Radio Shack box for a VCR that could run either on 110 Volts AC or 12 Volts DC.

That would be just the ticket for our truck. The fellow showed me the box and said that he needed $75 more than he needed a new VCR.

I said that I needed to see the actual VCR. As he kept talking, at one point I grabbed for the box and got hold of the end. I shook the box. It was very heavy and I realized that that box was far too heavy to have just a VCR inside.

I looked the fellow straight in the eye and shouted, "YOU GOT ROCKS IN THAT BOX DON'T YOU?" He threw the box onto the seat and told me to go to hell. He was screaming as he threw his car into gear and went tearing out of the parking lot.

At that point, it really hit me. I had almost paid real money for a VCR box filled with rocks!

A Riverboat & French Quarter

John Logan

After we found that it would cost $30 an hour to park our truck in New Orleans itself, we left our truck at the Mardi Gras Truck Stop with strong locks on both the trailer and truck doors. Jinny and I called a cab.

I have lots of images from the drive into New Orleans. We could see fairly large boats sunk down in the swamp muck. There were houses built in the swamp, sitting on stilts above the water. People living there had 'yards' that were an extended boat dock. Clean clothes are strung on a wire from the porch to a tree. A pulley is attached to the tree so that clothing can be moved from the porch to the other end of the line.

At one point, we saw an area where the ground was above the water, and it held a town complete with a fish processing plant.

The Muddy Mississippi

Lake Pontchartrain itself was filled with herons and egrets that came south to enjoy the abundant food supply of these waters. Then we started to see the tall buildings of New Orleans in the distance.

On the city riverfront, as we walked along a loud sound hit us in the ears. Looking in the direction of the sound, we saw a huge steam-powered stern-wheeler straight out of history. It was the Natchez—the boat that races the Delta Queen each year at St. Louis for bragging rights to being the fastest boat on the River.

My first thought was "I wish my father could be here." He grew up on the Ohio River and had told me about that riverboat sound from the time I was only knee high. We hurried along the riverside and got to the boat before it left the dock.

We bought tickets for a day cruise up the Mississippi, going around the crescent bend and up river into the area where a large number of ocean-going ships were docked.

These ships flew flags of many countries, but all also had an American flag flying to show respect for the nation where they were docked. Some were busy loading cargo and others unloading cargo from all parts of the world. New Orleans is one of the world's busiest ports.

Virginia & John
on the riverboat

I decided that I must see the big steam engines that pushed us along so quietly. When I got to the engine room I was welcomed and told to "enjoy but please don't touch because you could get burned on the hot parts of the engine."

Those two engines developed a couple thousand horsepower each. They moved slowly and were absolutely silent. Each engine had one piston tied to a push-rod that went through the backend of the boat and drove the large stern paddle wheel.

When he was a boy, my father used to help get sternwheelers started by climbing the rungs like a ladder until the steam engine would kick over a revolution on its own.

After we got off the boat, we walked in the direction of the French Quarter. In a park with very large, old trees, we came upon a man selling rides in his mule-drawn wagon. We told him that we needed a tour.

This turned into another adventure. The mule looked like he had traveled at least a hundred miles that day alone. His owner applied a 'persuader' so the mule would start off at a pretty good clip. Our driver rang the bells on the front of the buggy and gave us a tour of high spots in the French Quarter.

We saw the area where the battle of New Orleans, the final battle in the war of 1812, was fought. One story we heard said that the American soldiers grabbed a 'gator, filled him up with powder and shot, and touched off his behind!

When we got off the buggy, we made our way toward Bourbon Street, which was lined with restaurants, bars, strip joints, clip joints and blues bars. Enterprising people would set up a table and the proper ingredients to make drinks. Hawkers tried to get you to come into their establishments for drinks, food or sex.

Buildings in the French Quarter go back to the time that the French settled the area. In fact, building here involved the same swampy conditions as the location of Paris, France. The French dealt with that by constructing buildings on top of bales of cotton.

We found what looked like a good restaurant and were served crawdads, jambalaya, shrimp, and some gumbo—along with deep fried oysters that were out of this world.

The next day, we drove our truck to the south end of the delta, bobtailing along the river. Most of the time, we were actually below the level of the Mississippi river, with only sea walls and levees along the bank keeping the road dry.

At the end of the road was Venice, Louisiana, after which the road continued as a narrow strip of pavement, about as wide as the truck, going through a swamp.

We found a restaurant in Venice. I ordered a seafood combo that turned out to be the best I have ever eaten. That food was right out of the water into the frying pan.

New Orleans land is so close to the water level
that graves are built above-ground, as shown
by this picture

CHICKAMAUGA:

A CIVIL WAR DISCOVERY

John Logan

In a place called Chickamauga my life was altered.

Our trip had started in an ordinary way. We had picked up a load of cloth bundles in New Orleans, from a warehouse filled with bags of coffee beans and yard-goods from other countries. We had denim material that would be made into blue jeans. Our destination was a company located in Chickamauga, Georgia.

We worked our way north on Interstate 59 through Alabama, entering Tennessee at Chattanooga, driving around Lookout Mountain and turning south toward Chickamauga.

As we drove through south Chattanooga, we came to a large memorial to the 'Brave Men who Died during the Hostilities of the Civil War,' situated at the Georgia state line. I was aware that some serious fighting had taken place in this area. The Civil War had been a very emotional event for me since I was a very small child. Just thinking about it usually brought feelings of distress.

We didn't realize that we would go through a Civil War Battlefield on the way to our delivery at Chickamauga, Georgia. Very near that city, we saw a Memorial with piles of cannons and their balls on the sides of the roadway. Signs said that we were entering Fort Oglethorpe Chickamauga Civil War Battlefield Memorial.

The city of Chickamauga, a town dating back to pre-Civil War days, was just south of the battleground, and I could hardly wait to get our load of denim unloaded. I felt strongly that I had to get back into that battlefield.

The old factory where we delivered our load of yard-goods looked like it might have been there prior to the Civil War. The dock was at ground level, so a steep ramp had been dug down for the trailers to get lined up with the dock floor. The ramp was full of water and was too muddy for me to see its bottom.

I was concerned about backing into this ramp, but the receiving person on duty told me to just keep lined up with the door opening. I started backing down the ramp and the trailer fell into a deep and large hole in the bottom cement. To my horror, the whole trailer began to tilt over sideways.

I managed to get the trailer out of the hole, but only by the slimmest of margins. Then I jumped out, took a long piece of wood and stuck it into the hole to see how big and deep it really was. It turned out to be more than three feet deep and several feet long at the very edge of the cement.

Now that I knew the location of the hole, my second try was good and we got safely up to the dock. After we got our load off the trailer, our dispatch said we would have to wait it out until a load could be found in the area.

For once I was very happy to hear that because it would let us go back to the Chickamauga Battlefield! It didn't take me long to get the truck in gear and head north.

A few minutes later, we were once again looking at memorials to the brave men on both sides who fought and lost their lives.

I found a wide place along the roadway and pulled the truck over. We got out and started to walk around, with Jinny carrying our camera.

John standing by the Georgia memorial

As we walked further, up ahead of us was a large memorial dedicated to the soldiers of the State of Georgia. I began to read the inscriptions as Jinny walked on. A strange feeling came over me. I looked into the woods to the left of where Jinny was walking.

Suddenly, I was taken back to the battle!

I could smell the black gun powder permeating the air. I could hear the roar of cannon all around me and the constant crack of the small arms fire. I could hear munitions striking the trees and the sound of the trees splitting from the impact. Most of all I could feel the terror in the hearts of these brave men.

The cries and screams of the wounded and dying men echoed all around me. Tears were running down my face. Finally, I slumped down on the steps of the memorial. My spirit had gone back to this time of struggle between people who were as close as family members. Brothers fought against brothers and fathers ended up fighting against their sons.

Jinny finally saw that I was sitting on the steps in distress. She came over and I began to tell her what had just happened.

As we continued to walk around that battlefield, I knew I would never forget this place.

A couple of years later, I was in Las Vegas for a Thanksgiving dinner with both my brothers and their families. The discussion eventually got around to Chickamauga. One of them had a book about the Civil War, so we looked up the Battle, read and discussed all the information we could find.

My brother David and his wife Dena had been listening very carefully to the story of my experience at the battlefield, and they made a suggestion. They knew of a psychic named Jamison in Las Vegas who was said to be very good at telling a person about their past and future.

I decided to go see Jamison. He told me that I had been killed in a battle in the Civil War in the life just prior to this one. I looked at him and said "Chickamauga"? He said, "Yes"! Then he said I had been shot in the side and the arm. I was badly hurt but still trying to fight. Then the big one hit me square in the heart.

The psychic said that I had been in that battle and position because I had a driving urge to foster change among my fellow men.

I do know that I had an intense reaction to that place and that it was one of the places that have enlightened my spirit.

Stuck in Chester, California

John Logan

This story begins on a day when we delivered a load of mail boxes from Leigh Products in Coopersville, Michigan to Owens Distribution in Sparks, Nevada. That load was actually thousands of small packages, so it took most of the day to get them put away in the warehouse.

Then we listened to the weather forecast. We could see the clouds starting to roll over the top of the mountains to the west. One of the first weather-change indicators is a cloud formation that looks like a cereal bowl turned upside down. The movement of moisture combined with very high winds across the mountains makes that bowl.

Our next load of paper egg-cartons from Packaging Corporation was to be picked up at Red Bluff, California. That meant that we would have to 'deadhead' from Sparks, Nevada to Red Bluff, right over the Sierra Nevada mountains.

The radio forecast said the impending storm was going to be short but of high intensity. We knew that when the truck is empty, it's hard to get enough traction to move up or down steep mountain grades safely.

So we looked at the road map and decided we might beat the advancing weather system by going up Route 395. That would gradually take us to higher altitudes while running along the eastern edge of the mountain range to Susanville.

Near Doyle, we met strong winds that very nearly blew our tractor and trailer off the road. Further north the road went around a large dry lake bed called Honey Lake. We encountered wind gusts that several times caused the trailer to lift one side of its tires off the road surface.

These Sierra Mountains were formed when a very large block of the earth's crust broke and the eastern edge of the block rose skyward to an altitude of 10,000 feet in places. Magma from the earth's interior rushed through the fracture. The entire landscape on the eastern slopes of the Sierra is filled with beautiful and interesting volcanic lava flows.

As we went through Susanville, it was raining, so I hoped that just maybe we had beaten the main thrust of the storm.

When I hit the edge of town I changed to Route 36, a stretch that is one of our favorite roads. As we left Susanville, we started to climb up a steep mountain grade. From that road, on a clear day we could literally see for many miles back to the east. Going west we found ourselves entering a forest of trees so thick and tall that it felt as if we were in a tunnel.

It wasn't long before we noticed snowflakes, scattered at first, then coming down so thickly that it became hard to see the road. We were climbing at a slow but steady rate when the snow started to accumulate on the highway.

On Route 36, two mountain passes must be negotiated. First is Freedonyer Pass, then the pass that takes you over the shoulder of Mt. Lassen. As I approached Freedonyer, my windshield wipers were looking like ice-coated clubs.

I knew that the steep grade was going to continue for the next six to eight miles. There was no place to get off the road, let alone a place to turn around. So I also knew I had to keep moving.

My heart was right up in my throat. If I used too much throttle, the drive wheels would spin. With too little throttle pressure, the truck starts to lose momentum. I maintained my speed, despite passing other trucks that had stalled out.

After going around dozens of other vehicles, we finally topped out at the summit. That was a welcome sight! The giant trees were coated with so much snow that their limbs were hanging down. The whole world was covered with a blanket of snow.

When I started down the western side of the pass, the biggest problem was visibility and keeping our speed down. We were now entering a large basin area, within which is a beautiful lake called Almanor.

The town called Chester is located on the lakeshore, and we slowly drove down into the town. As we picked our way through town, the only people we saw were the local police and a snow plow working on a grocery store parking lot. Even the local bar was deserted.

On the west side of Chester, the road starts to climb again. It is gradual at first, then the grades get steeper and the road gets narrow and crooked. We came to the base of Morgan Summit and saw that the 'Chain Up' signs were up.

When we tried to chain up, it was impossible. But we had just passed a barn about a hundred yards back. Jinny and I walked back and saw that there was a chance of turning around. That was no simple task since it took both our eyes to see where the trailer was going in relationship to the roadway.

After several tries we made the barnyard backup, and, to our delight, the tractor was able to get enough traction to pull back out of the barnyard and onto the roadway. We started back east looking for a place to sit the storm out, and found ourselves again in Chester.

The snow was now at least a foot deep. We saw the local policeman and flagged him down to ask if there was any place that we could sit until morning. He said that the grocery store parking lot would be OK, so I drove into it. That got us off the main roadway and out of the way of snow plows who would be cleaning up the road in the morning—we hoped.

I spotted a payphone and called our dispatch office to tell them where we were. They told us to just stay put.

We were going to bed when someone knocked on the door of the truck. I jumped back up front and saw a very friendly man and woman standing there. They had been told by their neighbor, the policeman, about a truck from Grand Rapids, Michigan that was hung up in the storm.

The man asked if I had ever heard of a town called Cedar Springs, Michigan. I told him that we lived in Rockford and that I certainly knew Cedar Springs. When I said that our house was on a street called Summit Court, he said that he played in the hills and woods just north of us when he had been a young fellow growing up in Cedar Springs. Now he worked for IBM in a town just down below the mountains, but felt like he lived in heaven on earth in Chester.

We thanked them for being concerned and taking the time and effort to come downtown and talk with us. It made us feel we were actually among friends.

The next morning the sun shone through holes in the clouds. When the plows made their way past us, we pulled out right behind them and had no problem getting over the final pass and into the central valley.

This mountain and town are one of those places where you feel good just being alive and privileged to experience the beauty of people and nature.

Pushing the Edge

Virginia Logan

Our Westinghouse load to NASA Research Center at Edwards Air Force Base in California was followed by an experience of a major pressure on all truck-drivers: 'deliver on time.'

The base was in a large, high desert valley area. We were to deliver to the Test Facility Building. This flight research facility has played a leading role in the nation's aeronautical research from the space shuttle to unmanned combat vehicles. There was a museum where we purchased commemorative coins, one marking the Challenger tragedy on January 28, 1986.

When we called our dispatch center, they had a strange request: "Did we have enough hours available to get to Rocklin by 1 a.m. Pacific Time?" I had to do some quick figuring. It would be at least 60 miles east to Barstow, then about 450 miles to Rocklin. Since we were in California, I had to figure a 55 mph average for trucks, which meant at least 9 hours of driving. If we left Edwards AFB by 3:30 Pacific Time, that would give us 9 1/2 hours to get to Rocklin by 1 a.m.

Then I had to figure how many driving hours each of us had available. John had only 1 3/4 hours left, but I had 4 1/2 hours. After midnight we would both have 10 more hours available.

We could do it, so I called our dispatcher back to say "Yes, we can take that load." The first team had picked up a load of Herman Miller stock in Roswell, Georgia and gotten to Barstow, but was out of legal hours to continue on to Rocklin. We headed to Barstow and switched trailers. After eating with the other drivers at the Wild Horse Truck Stop, we headed wast.

Highway 58 is unique because its first stretch is a two-lane road across the flat high desert area with a lot of dips to accommodate the 'flood washes.' Next is Four Corners, where Route 58 crosses Highway 395. Then the road passes the 'Twenty Mule Team' Boron plant and Edwards Air Force Base. After that, it becomes a four lane divided highway.

We'd go up to Tehachapi Pass and stop at a DOT Truck Scale. From there on, it would be up and down until the final descent into Bakersfield and Highway 99 north.

We made it to Rocklin just on time.

Our dispatcher told us to drop that trailer, pick up an empty and head to Fremont for a load of Air Freight that wouldn't be ready until midnight. He also said that the Air Freight folks didn't want us spending the day at their dock.

We found a mall that provided places to eat and restrooms. We were pretty tired, so we found a shady spot to park under some trees, set the alarm and went to sleep.

About 10 p.m. Pacific Time, we drove to Air Freight. It was after midnight before we were loaded, but they still wanted the load at Land-Air in Indianapolis in 48 hours.

We decided to go the southern route, because it was April and our newspaper weather map showed possible storms across I-80. We fueled and stopped to eat at Kingman, Arizona. By the time we reached Cloverdale, Indiana (on the outskirts of Indianapolis), we both were close to 10 hours of driving for the day and tired.

But the push to deliver in 48 hours was strong. I drove on into Indianapolis and delivered our load by midnight. It was so close. I went for it.

Running on a Sheet of Ice

John Logan

Raton Pass, Colorado brings striking memories. We had a load of steel shelving that was being relocated from Los Angeles to Omaha, Nebraska. We were loaded to the maximum legal weight, which was normal when handling dense commodities.

To get from Los Angeles to Omaha you must get around the mountains. We always try to minimize miles, since we're only paid for miles estimated by a computer at our home base. We left California on Interstate 40 going through Arizona and New Mexico as far as Albuquerque.

There we jumped onto Interstate 25 to go around the bottom end of the mountains and still make our way northward. We went past Santa Fe, New Mexico in the dark. We didn't see the city but did realize that we were gaining altitude rapidly. In the moonlight, the outline of mesas appears. These are very tall and, in the dark, foreboding land features.

The truck was loaded full and heavy, and we were on unfamiliar highway, so Jinny was doing a lot of shifting. Every hill becomes a challenge to maintaining a reasonable speed while not becoming a traffic hazard.

We had been hearing about weather in the north as we crossed I-40, and were expecting to run into ice and snow at any time. We had clear sky and moonlight all the way north to the town of Raton, New Mexico. At that point we started to see some clouds appear in the northern sky.

Just short of the summit of Raton Pass, the roadway began to show signs of moisture and recent sanding operations. I took the wheel and within a couple of minutes I was going over the top of the pass. Some light misty raindrops began to hit the windshield when I started to descend the north side. Almost immediately, we were in a dense fog. Then I realized that I was running on a sheet of ice.

The ice was slick and so I had started down the incline slowly. Just touching the brakes could lock the wheels up, putting me totally out of control. I had barely enough traction to keep the truck going in a straight line and yet the force of gravity was taking me down faster and faster.

I thought about applying the engine retarder (the 'jake brake') to help take the pressure off the brakes. But even at the lightest setting, that could jack-knife the rig right over the side of the mountain.

I cut the power to the jake. The faster I went the more gears I had to shift up to keep the engine from over-revving.

I did a little praying. Finally the grade started to ease off and I felt I was regaining control. The fog was still thick, and the ice on the roadway was also still slick.

As I continued north I came to a Colorado D.O.T. scale. After driving over the scale, you have to park the truck and walk back to show your permits. The permits were OK, but I was barely able to keep my footing on the ice.

Happily, the road-grade had leveled off. It was slick but passable. I went a number of miles with only small grades to contend with. Then I came to a place called Colorado City. The road was flat and had been that way for the last twenty five miles. The rain was coming down at a good clip which made it hard to see the pavement. Here the road started to tilt downward and curved to the right.

Suddenly, my headlights were shining out into nothing but raindrops and fog.

As I straightened the truck out, I got a look at the debris and pieces of rock all over the roadway from earlier accidents. The grade was so steep I couldn't have stopped my heavy load even if it had been bone dry outside.

I applied the brakes as much as I could without sliding and losing control—and came to another curve going left. I kept the lightest touch possible on the brakes and feathered the steering.

At that point, again I couldn't see the pavement because the drop off from the edge of the curve was so steep. This time, fortunately, the pavement after the curve just went straight ahead.

I had tears in my eyes when I saw the bottom of the hill coming up. Thankfully, the roadway next did a sudden steep upgrade, and I used it to scrub off some of the speed.

As the road leveled out, the descent became gentle. At Pueblo, we reached the bottom of the hill and the end of the icy pavement.

My guardian angel, Gray-Otter, surely was with me.

Desert Dog

John Logan

We had just crossed the Utah Salt Flats and were headed into northern Nevada, when I discovered that I was out of smokes!

It was not very far to the Oasis Montello, where I exited the highway and drove in on a muddy road. I stopped the truck on a patch of gravel and started to walk over to the small store and restaurant.

There were large bushes on both sides of the doorway leading into the little store. When I got to within fifteen feet of the door something jumped out of the bushes. It was a dog with a very large flat head and a coat of wild fur that was like a calico cat.

He came straight for me! This animal had such a desperate look that I had visions of tearing pants and flesh.

He latched onto my leg! But, to my surprise, he didn't sink his teeth into my calf or knee. I looked down to see that he was holding onto my leg with his front legs for all he was worth.

After I realized that he wasn't interested in taking part of my leg with him, I reached down and patted him on the head. He responded to that like I was his last buddy in the world. He jumped up with muddy feet for more attention.

The owner of the store saw what had happened and came out to get the dog and apologize for the mess he had made of my pants. He said the dog was not his but belonged to a ranch about ten miles away. So he actually was a very scared, lost and lonely ranch dog.

This story has a sad ending because several months later at the beginning of the next winter I saw Desert Dog again. He had been hit by a car or truck and was lying along the interstate, dead.

I have gone through that Valley a couple of hundred times and I never fail to think about that Desert Dog.

Winter Desert Driving

A Log Cabin in Mendocino

John Logan

Along the west coast of Oregon, large amounts of rain fall year round. All plants grow like weeds. The forest is literally a rain-forest.

This story begins when a company called Holland Log Homes of Holland, Michigan received an order from a man in Mendocino, California who was going to build a log home on a mountaintop above the city. The trees were cut on the West Coast and shipped to Michigan for sawing and shaping. Then we trucked them back west to a location only a few hundred miles from where they had grown.

We were asked by our dispatcher if we would like to take a load going to Mendocino, California. We'd never been to the coast in that area, so we said "Sure, why not?"

We came into the San Francisco Bay area on Interstate 80, then crossed the San Rafael Bridge and turned north on Highway 101. We were soon surrounded by high rolling hills, part of the mountain coastal range. We were driving in the early morning darkness and so the real impact of what was to come had not become apparent.

We went through a small town called Cloverdale, California. It was the last town along Route 101 before we would start west on a very narrow road on which two trucks passing each other had to watch so they didn't hit each other's mirrors.

The roadway was crooked, narrow, and steep. People lived in houses built at the very edge of the road and extending out over the mountainside. Seeing this made us realize why we heard about houses sliding down the mountainsides in California.

We were breaking over the top of the mountain at the first light of day, and the downhill grade was steep and crooked. The speed limit was reduced to 25 mph; some of the hairpin turns were signed-down as low as 15 mph.

I had shortened my wheel base as much as the equipment would allow because I was expecting some pretty narrow and curvy road ahead, but I had underestimated the curves.

Sign: 9% grade ahead,
a drop of 9 feet for
every 100 feet traveled.

Curves to the right were no problem because I could use road space to keep the trailer off the cliff face. But to turn left, I'd have to enter the curve hugging the ditch along the cliff face, then maintain the close distance to the rock cliff all the way around the hairpin turn. My eyes jumped from the rocks that we were missing by inches to the trailer that was close to falling off the mountainside behind us.

It was a relief to reach the bottom of that first mountain and run through a valley filled with farms, vineyards and a little town.

Soon we started to see redwood trees along both sides of the roadway. After we went through Boonville, the trees started to get very thick.

We drove into Hendy Woods State Park, which is second growth redwood. The trees were growing in circles around the stumps of the harvested virgin redwood forest, some right along the edge of the pavement. The forest was so dense that we had to turn on the headlights to see the roadway clearly in some places.

Tree limbs grew out over the roadway, so close to the trailer roof that I was brushing through them as we drove along. I saw huge tree stumps, one so large that someone had built a small hut on top of it.

We popped out of the forest to go through a little hamlet called Navarro, California. Then we headed back into trees, where the roadway followed a small stream called Navarro Creek. Small glimmers of sunlight filtered down through the forest canopy and illuminated the creek bed.

Continuing westward, we descended into a valley with steep sides. Navarro Creek was considerably larger now and had, over time, cut itself a rather deep valley.

At the forest's edge, we were between two high mountains, driving along the water's edge where logs were piled in huge heaps. They had been washed downstream during floods and deposited at this point near the ocean, where they were left.

At the top of one hill, the roadway leveled out and we were running on a plateau that ran along the ocean. It must have been a three to four hundred feet drop straight down to the beach. I saw a big buck deer standing on the edge of the drop-off, totally oblivious to our presence as he looked out across the ocean waters.

To this day, that image remains vivid in my mind.

Our directions told us to now look for a road marked Comptche-Ukiah Road. We were to make a right hand turn which would take us back to the east; after two and a half miles, we were to look for a utility pole with the number 42501 painted on a small sign.

At that pole I was to turn left onto the small private road going north. The building site for the log cabin was supposed to be the fourth driveway on the left.

We turned right and went east-bound on Comptche-Ukiah Road. It immediately started up a very steep grade where the pavement was so shaded by trees that it was covered with slick green moss.

The truck's drive-wheels were on the edge of spinning for the entire way up the grade. We broke out of the trees at the top of the hill. Jinny was keeping an eye on the tele-phone poles and I was keeping a keen eye on the tree limbs. We final-ly found the pole with number 42501 painted on it. It was the top sign, with barely visible numbers.

The private road to the left was right where the directions said it would be. But our truck was wider than the road. In fact, the road disappeared into the forest only a few hundred feet from its entrance.

After some wriggling around, I managed to get the trailer backed into the driveway and off the main road.

We sat there for quite a while, with no one in sight. Then we walked a long way back into the woods, still finding no one. We saw tracks showing that other trucks had tried, unsuccessfully, to get back into the building site. Trees along the narrow road were marked with truck hits on their bark.

We walked back to our truck and waited. Finally, a pick-up truck drove up. The driver wanted to know if we had the logs for their new house from Holland, Michigan.

We told them that we did, but it was impossible to get our truck in through the trees. What was needed was a small truck capable of negotiating the driveway through the woods. So they went off to find help.

Sometime later, they returned with several friends and their pick-up trucks. One truck had a large rack which was needed for the longer pieces inside our trailer.

They had worked for a couple of hours transferring logs, when we decided to unhook from our trailer and get something to eat in Mendocino.

Mendocino, California, whose original settlers came from Russia, is a cross between a Russian and an early American town. The entire town sits on the top of a neck of land, called Cape Mendocino, which juts out into the Pacific Ocean.

The ocean waves have cut into the shore so deeply that it is literally a vertical cliff down to the water for most of the way around the city. In one place, I saw a gradual slope allowing people to safely get down to the water's edge. At the bottom of that slope was a small harbor facility with a limited number of docks.

Mendocino had small tourist shops and unusual restaurants. We picked one that was built on the top of an old building so it gave us a view out over the ocean.

We had a good breakfast and looked in some of the shops. We visited a store with telescopes of all sizes and kinds. I found one that looked good and pointed it out across the little bay. I could see a beautiful beach at the bottom of the cliffs and some huge tracks in the sand going from the water's edge to the cliffs and back to the water's edge.

I asked the store owner about the tracks and he said it looked like an elephant seal had hauled himself out of the water to preen his fur.

We returned to our trailer just as the people were finishing the unloading. We asked permission to walk back into the forest to see where they were going to build their log home. We knew we were getting close to the building site when we saw a big shaft of light streaming down onto the forest floor. The owners had cut just enough trees to allow for building of the house and a storage building. Otherwise the forest had been left undisturbed.

Virginia on the forest road

Such a place of natural beauty makes me feel small and insignificant. This thick forest was totally silent except for an occasional small bird that would land close and look you over. I felt at peace with Mother Nature and God.

The owner told me that the temperature only varies about five to eight degrees from its normal 60 degrees during the entire year. If there is a down side to this place, it is that it is one of the most active earthquake areas that you could find in the United States. They were taking great precautions to build their new home so that it would stand up to the shaking of the frequent earthquakes in the area.

The owner also said that this area had been owned by a man from Grand Rapids, Michigan, whose name was Blodgett. He had purchased this California land because of the vast fortune he could make from logging the huge redwood trees.

The loggers would set a fire that completely burned all the brush and hardwood trees out of the forest. That gave them easy access to the redwood. Because the trees here were so straight and large, they produced raw lumber that could be used for almost any purpose. If a tree was not quite straight it was cut down and burned to get it out of the way!

Today most of the forest is second growth, and vulnerable because trees spring up from the sucker roots of the old tree stumps, roots that are just under the surface. People walking on them can kill them.

It was time for us to leave this wonderful mountain top. We descended, went north and then turned back east, heading to Fort Bragg, California.

A Lady New to Mountain Driving

John Logan

For 125 miles, running from the west side of Denver all the way to Vale, Colorado, a more beautiful and dangerous place to handle a heavy load would be hard to find anywhere in the continental U.S.

The Eisenhower Tunnel goes through the Rocky Mountains a thousand or more feet below the Loveland Pass. Jinny and I were coming out of this tunnel on a day with bright sunshine and no wind. Big trucks are instructed by large signs to 'gear down.' The speed limit is reduced to no more than 25 miles an hour. Signs say '6% grade ahead for the next six miles.' They are not kidding.

A 6% grade is a drop of six feet for every one hundred feet traveled. Westbound out of the Eisenhower Tunnel the road has six miles of 6% grade without any let-up.

I had geared down as I started. Jinny and I were talking about what wonderful day we had going for us, when I noticed a small truck sitting next to the runaway ramp about a half mile ahead. A lady next to the truck was waving her arms wildly and obviously crying. I came to a stop directly behind her truck.

She ran up to say that she had lost her brakes. This lady had packed all her belongings into the small Budget rental truck she was driving and had put her automobile on a trailer behind it. Then she had filled the car full of items that wouldn't fit in her truck. Her rig was definitely overloaded.

She had started in Minnesota on her way to Las Vegas, Nevada. When I asked why she had chosen this route, she said the map showed it as the shortest way to get from point A to Point B.

I asked if she had ever been in the mountains before, and she said 'No!' Then I asked if anyone had explained proper procedures for mountain driving. Again, she responded with a definite 'NO!' She also said it had taken her two days to reach this point that was just two hours west of Denver.

Remembering our driving-trainer, Big Mac, I explained several facts. First, you must check the brakes and adjust them if needed. Second, your speed must be controlled.

As we talked, she kept begging me to take her truck down the mountain. I told her that I definitely would not do that for her. But I did tell her that I would make it possible for her to do it herself, safely—and to then continue on with the many hundreds of hills between where she was and Las Vegas.

First I checked her brakes. They were working well. Then I told her to put the 5-speed truck in second gear, and not to take it out of that gear for any reason.

Next, I told her that she could use the brakes, but for only one reason: to keep control of her speed. I told her that she must be careful not to push them too hard because they will get hot and lose their ability to either slow or stop her. If she kept the truck speed slow and safe she would be just fine until she got to Silverton, Colorado.

I explained the many grades to come and how to handle the worst of them. She finally settled down enough to give it a try.

She gave me a huge bear-hug along with a grateful little kiss and started off down the mountain.

I went on down the mountain ahead of her. I kept tabs on her with the CB radio and found that she was doing just fine. I continued to listen for any problems as I put distance between us. She was still doing fine as I went over the top of the next grade. I never heard from her or saw her again. I hope her new life and job in Las Vegas worked out far beyond her hopes and dreams.

It all comes down to gravity, your vehicle, and you as the operator. Your own life and the lives of others are in a driver's hands.

John working on his truck

NEBRASKA SNOW STORMS

Virginia Logan

It was January, 1993, and we started the year with a load of furniture to California State University in San Marcos, California. We traveled our usual route across I-80 to Salt Lake City, Utah, then followed I-15 south to San Marcos.

The San Marcos and San Diego area had 70 degree temperatures, warm sunshine, and people jogging in shorts—a treat for folks from Michigan in January.

After our delivery was unloaded, we had to lay over until the next day. The San Diego area is wonderful for tourist and sunbirds, but not truckers. There is a very nasty truck stop at National City that has a fence around it. They lock the gate at night, so truckers have to park outside the fenced area and be hassled by 'lot-lizards,' CB slang for local prostitutes.

The only decent truck stops are about 120 miles east on I-8 at El Central and about 100 miles north to Ontario. Since we were already north of San Diego, we decided to just head up to Ontario for the night.

Dispatch had told us we were to stay in the delivery area, but we expected to be told to head north to Fremont, California, 475 miles from our delivery point.

We were indeed ordered to Fremont, where our first pick-up was four bins of automotive parts from a Toyota plant. We knew that we were supposed to pick up an additional item from Sacramento to fill the truck, but the Toyota plant wasn't supposed to know that. We also knew that there wasn't going to be enough room for the second item unless one of these huge bins was double-stacked. But Toyota always sealed its load before it left the plant.

John managed to convince the packer to do the double stacking and let us out without sealing the load. We headed for Sacramento.

The second item was a 1967 Chevy Camero. We were supposed to meet someone in a parking lot and they would have this car on a trailer so that it could just be pushed right into our trailer. They did arrive. With many shoves and pushes the car rolled into our trailer. They nailed down pieces of wood to block the car on all sides and we used straps both front and back.

By the time we were finished, it looked pretty secure. We had to make out our own bill of lading, which was unusual.

Now we were ready to roll. Donner Pass was easy and the load was light, so we hoped to make some time. On across Nevada, Utah, and Wyoming—we were doing great.

John was driving as we entered Nebraska and it was snowing. When he turned the shift over to me, he warned me of possible blinding conditions at times from the dry powdery snow. Add a 30 mph north wind and about 6 inches of snow in the left lane.

I got past Big Springs, Nebraska, with the easy levels of traffic. Then along came a trucker with a black trailer that couldn't stand the slower speed in the right lane. ZOOM—he went on by and I was blinded by the snow he threw up!

If he had moved right on over into the right lane, it would have been OK. But he stayed on the left, and even though I slowed down, I couldn't get out of his trail of blinding snow.

This was scary. "I have to hold the wheel straight and slow down some more," I told myself. Suddenly I could see, but only to realize that I was headed into the median.

John was in the sleeper when I screamed "I'm going in the ditch," so that he could brace himself for whatever was to come.

He said later that he had felt the slow-down and unusual tilt, so he was already hanging on.

Luckily it was a fairly level and wide median. So I kept my foot on the pedal and started feathering the truck back toward the highway. Soon John poked his head out of the sleeper for a look and couldn't believe his eyes. I was back up on the highway.

About this time, I could hear a voice over the CB saying "Mill Creek, Mill Creek: are you OK? Saw you go into the median after I passed you." I grabbed the mike and yelled that I was back up on the road, but that I was blinded when he passed me and he should slow down. He said that the reason he was passing was that everyone was going so slow.

In snowy conditions you can't pull off on the unplowed shoulder. Add the fact that Rest Areas are always packed at night and especially in this weather. So I just kept going.

I checked all the gauges, found that everything appeared normal—I wasn't shaking too much either.

Then, not far down the road, I saw three 4-wheelers off in a deep ditch on the right. Pretty soon I heard another trucker cussing out the same truck that had passed me. Sure enough, truck-tracks were headed off into the median.

Somehow the fact that some other driver ended up in the median made me feel better, so I kept going, looking for a spot to safely get off the road. I remembered that I'd be coming to the North Platte Weigh Station soon. They are always open, so I'd pull off there and check things over.

This time, when I came to the Weigh Station, the sign said "CLOSED.' But there was some activity on the scale. Sitting there was the truck with a black trailer, the one that had sent me and another trucker off the road—AND the weigh master was making the driver get out of his truck!

They do listen to the CB, so maybe there would be some justice served here after all.

I was still looking for a safe place to exit when another truck came by—Whoosh! This one pulled back into the right lane, but I was shaking now and knew that I had to get off the road.

I pulled into the next Rest Area and sat there staring at the wind blowing the snow drifts around the truck in front of me. After a half hour or so, I realized I should check the truck over.

So I got my coat, gloves, and flashlight and climbed out in knee-high drifts. I wiped the snow off the lights and checked everything I could, and found nothing wrong. I couldn't bring myself to open the trailer doors in that wind, so any questions about the load would just have to wait for answers.

After another hour, the wind seemed to be letting up, so I ventured back out on the road and continued my shift.

The next day, we looked in the trailer in the day-light and nothing had moved. It was all secure!

Danger-Hazmat!

John Logan

One of the most uncomfortable situations a trucker must face is being in close proximity to hazardous materials. At times, you get a dispatch that is actually hazardous to your health. I can think back to three times when I felt very uneasy about our personal safety.

The first incident happened in the Los Angeles area. We had been dispatched to pick up a load of furniture. It was early in the day when I pulled into the plant for the pickup. We stopped at the security shack and were told to drive along the side of the plant to where the docks were located at the back corner of the building. As I got near that back corner, I noticed a number of chemical tanks marked with hazardous material labels.

The loading area was quite small and arranged so that a trucker had to squirm around just to get his truck up to the dock. At that point, we were told that our load wasn't going to be ready for several hours.

We had been sitting for a couple of hours when we heard the musical horns of a Roach Coach (a catering truck, usually for outdoor workers). We were getting hungry, so we jumped down from our truck and headed toward the food service truck.

We had only walked about twenty yards from our truck when we came to the tanks of chemical agents that I had noticed when we drove into the loading dock. I now took the time to read the Hazmat Labels and the warning signs that were posted on the wall next to the tanks. It said that no employee or person was allowed to walk up to these deadly tanks.

We got something to eat and continued to sit at the dock for several more hours. This gave me a chance to start to think about the position I was in and the possible ramifications if something went wrong. Those tanks were filled with Cyanide.

The second dangerous occasion happened some months later along the south coast of Texas. We had been dispatched to a petrochemical plant at Wadsworth, Texas. It was early in the morning and had been raining. The air was filled with thick fog making it hard to see the highway.

We were running on relatively narrow roads and headed in the direction of the coast. When we arrived at the plant entrance, it was so obscured by the fog that we drove on by. So we started looking for a turn-around spot.

A couple more miles down the road, I came to a parking area where cars and boat trailers were parked. Beyond this parking area was the beach and the Gulf of Mexico. I snaked my way through the parked vehicles and got turned around.

I was very careful not to miss the plant entrance on the second try. We made our turn into the plant and followed the signs directing us down a roadway around the outer edge of the property.

I finally came to a sign which I interpreted to mean that shipping was straight ahead. As we continued, the roadway was getting narrower. Then I noticed that there were ponds on both sides of our truck. The road made a sharp turn to the right—and we encountered a DANGER sign: "No unauthorized persons permitted in this area." I couldn't turn around or back up in that thick fog.

The next sight was chilling. An 'authorized person' with a long stick in his hands was stirring the steaming contents of the pond we were driving next to. HE was wearing a very expensive gas mask affair which covered his entire head and upper body.

We kept on driving and finally found the security office, located some distance from the shipping docks. They gave us hard hats and a pamphlet about safety procedures inside the plant grounds. It told us if we at any time heard a specific number of blasts on a very loud horn to run to the nearest equipment locker, put on a gas mask, and run to a designated safe zone.

That seemed a bit much to expect of a complete stranger to the plant. We were glad to get loaded and leave.

The third incident took place in a small town just outside of New Orleans. The product we were picking up was not hazardous. We reported into the guard shack. They sat us down in front of a television to watch a movie which had been especially prepared for the benefit of visitors. It explained the chemicals and the problems that arise if an accident should happen while we were on the company property.

After we had watched the movie we were asked to sign a number of forms that stated that we understood the risks and the emergency procedures. Then we were handed hard hats and small emergency breathing devices. Here too we were told that if we heard a very loud blast on the big warning whistle to head up wind and vacate the property. They said our life might depend on our following their instructions.

We sat for some time on the roadway which leads to the shipping docks. They had a small lake for emergency water reserves in the case of a fire breaking out in the plant. I noticed that every employee was working with the same equipment on their person that we had been issued.

During the loading, I asked one employee how he dealt with the dangers of working in this place. He said that after a while he just didn't think about it. He certainly wasn't paid extra because of the danger.

I would rather drive through a snow storm than work inside a hazardous materials environment.

California Poppies

John Logan'

We were waiting for a dispatch in a truck stop in Ontario, California. This truck was equipped with satellite communication with our home base, and our dispatcher told us to start north into the central valley of California, where we'd be told the details about our load.

We took Interstate 15 to Route 138. This is where the San Andreas Fault makes a turn and goes around the north side of the San Gabriel Mountains. Here the crust of the earth has been twisted and broken by that fault line. Huge broken rock slabs have been thrust vertically up into the air on their edges.

Land along the San Andreas Fault

People do live here, some on small farms. I recall one farm that had what looked like thousands of white domestic ducks wandering all over land.

For a short time we drove through a valley. Then the narrow road began to climb steeply. Because trucks use this road a lot, there are turn off places along the grade.

When you break over the top you are looking out onto the High Desert in an area called Antelope Valley. You can see for 70 to 80 miles to the northwest from this point.

This area has little communities along both sides of its length through the Antelope Valley. Whatever you might like to buy is for sale somewhere in the shops and open-air market along this road.   War Surplus, Antiques, Produce, Live Puppies, Cars, Trucks, Restaurants, and Land Sales are just a few of the signs.

After about 30 miles of Joshua trees and shops of every description we arrived in Palmdale, California. It and its neighbor, Lancaster, are involved in Aero Space Technology. The Stealth Bomber was built and unveiled here. Years earlier, I'd visited the Aero Space Museum in Palmdale with my brothers. I had a chance to walk up to a SR-71 Black Bird and put my hands on the edge of its wing.

On the northwest side of Lancaster, the road flattens out and we started to see clumps of orange-red California poppies. Clumps grew together, and soon we were looking at areas solidly colored with poppies. We were about 15 miles away from the Tejon Pass when it felt as if the whole world was covered with California poppy magic (picture at right).

It was a fragrant fairyland of flowers, a place that raised your spirit and left you with a wonderful warm feeling. As we arrived in Gorman, a small town located near the summit of the Tejon Pass, to our delight the flower show continued.

Canadian Rockies & Flood Relief

Virginia Logan

In May, we had the good fortune to get a load of Haworth office systems headed to Vancouver, British Columbia, Canada. We crossed into Canada at Blaine, Washington, where we had to buy a temporary B.C. permit. The Canadian official joked that the B.C. meant 'bring cash.'

The load was delivered to a building right in the Metro area so we were able to walk around, observe, and take pictures. It was a warm sunshiny day in a beautiful city with huge flowers everywhere.

We ate in an outside cafe and later watched as a Harbor Air Transport plane took off from the water in the harbor. When we returned to where the installers were unloading our truck in the street, the consignee remarked 'Oh no, now we're attracting tourists!'

The installers looked over at us and laughed. 'That's the truck drivers.'

Virginia in Vancouver, BC

We got our next dispatch: a 'deadhead' to Calgary, Alberta to pick up a load in the morning for Xerox. That meant driving over the Canadian Rockies! We followed the Fraser River Valley and saw 'Hells Gate' where the river comes rushing through a very narrow passage. It was spring, so the river was definitely speeding along.

On through Kamloops, then we stopped at a lookout point in the Glacier National Park. It was about 2 a.m. and pitch dark so we couldn't see much. We left telling ourselves that we'd return for a daylight visit.

We drove on through the rugged mountains between Golden and Lake Louise, where John did get a picture of our truck with the mountains just at dawn and just past the area where the winter Olympics were in Calgary. We found our destination and even had a couple of hours to rest.

Mountain at dawn near Calgary, Canada

At Sweetgrass, Montana, we crossed back into the U.S. It was while driving in North Dakota that we got a call telling us that our son Jason had been in the emergency room in Ann Arbor for 6 hours. Luckily the problem was taken care of without surgery.

Later in the same year, just as we were driving from Los Angeles through Utah, we had a message over our communications satellite. My sister Elizabeth told us that our daughter Marie was in the hospital. We made it back to Milwaukee before Marie was released from the hospital, so I got a flight from Milwaukee to Detroit Metro, and arrived at the University Hospital in time to help Marie return to her apartment. John finished the trip to Michigan.

One Great Plains storm to remember happened in eastern Nebraska. We had stopped in Atlantic, Iowa, for a bite to eat and when we headed west there were reports of a tornado just to the south of our location. We watched the skies and listened to the local radio station. Since that tornado was heading northeast and we were driving west, we did manage to drive out of the danger area

We also delivered a load for the American Red Cross Flood Relief program. The load of cleanup kits was picked up at the Salvation Army in Los Angeles and delivered to the Salvation Army in St. Louis. The location in St Louis was just down a closed street from where propane tanks were floating in their cradles, a dangerous situation.

We talked with a student who had come from New York to help out—and saw lines of people waiting to get volunteer applications in. We were just one of hundreds of trucks delivering relief items to this location.

Fire in the Mountains

John Logan

The unexpected is the order of the day when you are a trucker. We had unloaded in the Los Angeles Basin and were dispatched to the Central Valley. It was time to call the shipper for instructions and directions. This load was no exception to the normal rule of shippers: 'Hurry up, you are late. Then wait till your load is actually ready.'

We drove north, around the western end of Los Angeles, then past the edge of the Beverly Hills and over the Sepulveda Pass. After the Pass, it is a quick descent into the San Fernando Valley. On a clear day, you are looking down into an area where millions of people live.

At the Valley's north side, we came to San Fernando, California, and the San Gabriel and Santa Susana mountains. At the point where Route 14 had exited I-5, major earthquake damage had been done to the road. This is the spot where a California highway patrolman lost his life by running his motorcycle into mid-air, where moments before there had been a large bridge.

We descended on I-5 for a short distance into another valley. Then we started a gradual climb, and at the town of Castaic, we knew that the road began a long, steep 6% grade, running for several miles with no let up in the angle of ascent. If a truck is loaded, it can be a long, slow climb to the top.

On this day, the road was congested. As we came to Castaic, the traffic was stopped. Police were not allowing anyone to climb the mountain and we could see smoke billowing up from the mountain side ahead. Wildfire!

I turned on the CB Radio so Jinny and I could listen to the CB conversations and she could check the map for options. Someone said that there was an old road built prior to the Interstate that might offer a way to circumvent the fire. When Jinny checked the map, it didn't look like a wise decision.

We thought we'd sit the fire out and proceed after the Interstate was reopened. Since we were hungry, we exited the Interstate and drove into the town of Castaic, where we discovered that we were not alone in our decision.

After finding a curb place near a McDonald Restaurant, we decided that we could be stuck for some time and that, along with eating, it was important to let our customer know about our situation.

We also continued to listen to the CD chatter. Someone said he was in a big truck and had just come over the only route available to get around the fire. The trucker told us that the Ridge Road was all gravel but in pretty good shape.

We got directions for finding Ridge Road, and decided to give it a try. It curved around like a snake trail. When we looked out as we went around a sharp turn, it was hundreds of feet straight down to the first bounce. The traffic was heavier than this roadway was ever intended to handle.

View of the mountain fire from a distance

From up on this high ridge, we could see the fire wildly burning its way higher and higher into the ridges. The sage brush that covered these mountains was dry from months with very little rain. That made it an explosive fire.

Smoke was coming up the mountain in such thick clouds that it was hard to breath. We closed all outside ventilation in an attempt to keep the acrid smoke out of our truck.

The California Dept. of Forestry had dispatched all kinds of equipment to fight the flames. We saw helicopters with fire-retardant chemicals and water-bomber airplanes attack the fire. Firemen on the ground were using bulldozers and four-wheel-drive vehicles to get into the flames.

We knew we were watching some courageous and skilled people doing a dangerous job. The fire did finally gave way to the pressure of these well trained and brave men.

When we rejoined Interstate 5, we were north of the flames and almost completely clear of the acrid smoke. We were then traveling through a high valley, with mountain peaks still towering over our heads. Rock on both sides of the valley had been folded into a vertical direction. It is old sea-bottom thrust up out of the ocean to the top of these folded mountains.

This area gets strong winds, so many wind turbines are generating electricity. The air itself is clean and sweet-smelling because it has just blown in from the ocean.

As we continued, the grade got steep enough that we had to start downshifting. At the end of our climb, we reached Tejon Pass, named for the Tejon family who settled this area. That family still has a large ranch located in these picturesque mountain tops.

On the descent, we drove past Frazier Park and Lebec, California. Large signs with flashing lights appeared to tell truckers to pull into the brake-check area and make certain their brakes are working properly. The speed limit is then reduced to a maximum of 35 mph.

The highway then started down a very steep grade with highway patrolmen stationed along the way to enforce that speed limit. This was the famous Grapevine Grade, named after the Grapevine Canyon where wild grapes still grow. The city of Grapevine is located at the bottom of the grade.

This mountain has seen some terrible truck accidents. Trucks usually run nose-to-tail down this grade, and no passing is allowed.

The Grapevine Grade, California

The highway patrol knows all the driving patterns of this canyon road, and they sit at the bottom of the mountain looking for speeders and people with their brakes on fire. I have been told that it is a very expensive matter.

Near the bottom of the Grapevine, you can see for miles over the San Joaquin Valley, where enough food is grown to feed nearly the entire population of the United States.

Driving the Pecos Trail

John Logan

In 1996, we had the chance to travel the Pecos Trail, which for hundreds of years has run through some of the most desolate yet beautiful Southwest country.

We started at Fort Stockton, Texas, where an 8-foot tall roadrunner statue named Pete catches the traveler's eye (right: image of the fierce roadrunner). Going south on route 285 out of Fort Stockton takes you into brush country. There is very little soil here. Most of what you see is rock and thick brush. The land gets little rain, but lots of intense sunshine. We saw lots of  animals, both ranch and wild: cattle, horses, sheep, goats and deer.

Jinny and I had a delightful experience one afternoon when a family of pigs crossed the highway in the distance ahead of our truck. First we saw a large pig come out of the brush on the right side of the road. It stopped in the middle of the road and stood on the white line to look left and then right and see if it was safe for a road crossing.

This pig then looked back to where it had come from and snorted. To our surprise, a long line of little baby pigs appeared, marching nose-to-tail toward the mother pig.

When the first little pig got to his mother she immediately started to lead them to the other side of the roadway. Then a second mother pig came out leading another parade of little pigs.

She also stopped on the white line as the little ones behind her continued to file past her. When the last little pig got to the middle of the roadway, the mother took one last look back into the brush. She waited till the last little pig got under the fence and then proceeded to follow.

By the time our truck got to the spot where they had gone under the fence, they were hidden. We were impressed with their training and strict obedience while making that dangerous crossing of a public highway. It's hard to get an eyeball on a wild hog, let alone a look at two families of them.

Proceeding south, we ran through deep washes. This land is baked as hard as a rock, but over millions of years, rain water did wash through, cutting valleys or canyons. The road runs straight down the side of the canyon, across the bottom, then straight up the other side. It makes for a roller-coaster ride. If your load is heavy, it also makes for some tricky shifting as you climb the canyon-side.

It was interesting to look for the unusual signs at the entrance to ranches. I remember one die-cast metal sign that had a running cow with a rope tied around its neck. At the end of the rope was a cowboy attempting to catch the critter. Just below that scene was the name of the ranch owner.

After Sanderson Canyon is the town of Sanderson, Texas, a little cow-town straight out of the history books. It is a mixture of Mexicans, Mexican Americans, and Anglo-Americans. It has some good Mexican restaurants and more than a couple cowboy bars, along with a Justice of the Peace and local court building.

As we climbed up out of the Sanderson Canyon, the roadway started to cross an area just north of the Rio Grande River. Some of the ranchers here seemed to be prospering and some were struggling.

In this area, one day we came upon a tiny little goat. He had gotten through a fence and was on the edge of the pavement. His mother was standing inside the fence trying to get her kid to crawl back through the fence. He saw us and heard the loud noise of our truck. That sent him into a panic, so he started running as fast as he could make his little legs run toward the fence line. He must have been looking at his mother and ignoring the fence. As we went by, that little goat hit the fence at full speed.

Here, every wash and canyon leads to the Rio Grande. The hills are fairly large and rolling. We climbed to a place called Eagles Nest, where rain water running down a wash had cut through the cap rock layer of the bedrock and started working on the softer limestone layer beneath.

The result was a deep but narrow canyon, with a series of natural shelves of rock.

Continuing along the Rio Grande, we came to a little town called Langtry, Texas. Yep! It was the home of Judge Roy Bean, who in the old days was the only 'Law West of the Pecos.' Today there is a museum and saloon along with a handful of houses.

A few miles to the east, the road comes to the Pecos River, which itself has cut a deep canyon through the rock on its way to the Rio Grande. A parking area and a tourist overlook are up where the highway bridges the canyon. Unfortunately, our truck was too large to pull into this facility, so we had to be happy with a quick look at the canyon as we crossed the bridge.

East of the Pecos, we saw the Amistad Reservoir and Dam. The economic effects of the Amistad Dam are readily visible in the campgrounds and marinas that take care of fisherman.

At Del Rio, Texas, we turned on Route 277, leaving the parched and sun-baked land and beginning to see green foliage. The rain lets people grow produce here, along with lots of pecan trees. Some farms have large groves of nut trees.

Route 277 passes through several small farm towns before it comes to Eagle Pass, Texas, where a bridge gives people access into Mexico. Hunters cross the border here in quest of large deer and wild boar. I was told that the adventure begins when sportsmen cross the river. They need a reputable hunting guide, because they are moving into an area with no law-enforcement.

To the southeast, still on Route 277, ranchers have erected very tall fences around their property. These guest ranches offer sportsmen an opportunity to hunt for exotic animals from all over the world. I have heard that some of the animals have come from such exotic places as a city zoo.

The brush in this part of Texas is so thick it is impossible to see more than a couple of hundred feet. It is also infested with cactus plants that grow only several feet high. This makes it nearly impossible to hunt deer on foot, so local people use four-wheel-drive vehicles with a high platform or a portable hunting platform to scout for deer.

Driving on through rolling hills and thick brush country, we have seen the national bird of Mexico, a fierce predator with beautiful markings called a caracara. Seeing these birds always gave us a feeling of being blessed.

It is not far to I-35 where we turned south to the town of Laredo, Texas. Since the North American Free Trade Agreement, this town has been like a well watered weed.

I am pro-American and pro-Mexican, but I also see that the rules are not the same on both sides of the border. Americans get the products, but Mexicans seem to have gotten the jobs. When we'd sit waiting for a train to pass, the railcars were filled with the products headed north.

A Texan Military Experience

John Logan

Carrying a load of goods to a United States military base is always an adventure. This time we were taking furniture to an Air Force Base in Wichita Falls, Texas, located just inside the northern border of Texas and straight south of Oklahoma City, Oklahoma.

We took Interstate 44 south from Oklahoma City, a stretch of highway near a lot of construction and about as rough a road as an Interstate can get.

When I say it was rough, I do mean rough. We were driving the best equipment in the trucking industry, with air-ride suspension on both the tractor and the trailer. But the bumps in this highway were so bad that, if you were trying to sleep behind the driving seats, you bounced into the air. If you were driving, you weren't certain of not smashing your head on the roof of the tractor.

After a lot of that bouncing, we arrived at the Wichita Air Force Base Security Gate and Office. They had us pull our truck over to the side of the entrance gate. The security guards took our paperwork and, with a phone call, found the contact person who confirmed that we were expected. Then the guards had to open the trailer to confirm that we were indeed hauling furniture.

We were met by our contact person, who led the way to the building where this furniture was to be installed. The delivery place was surrounded with high fences and very serious looking guards who had their rifles loaded and at the ready.

Our contact person talked to the staff on duty at this guard shack, giving them the paperwork for our load and explaining what we needed to do. It took quite a bit of talking to further authorities before we were granted clearance to actually enter.

We were told to proceed, but under no circumstances to get outside our truck. For a restroom, we were to ask for and then follow a security guard. I opened the doors of our trailer and then backed through the gate. After more discussions, a doorway that led into the heart of the building was picked.

We did use the restrooms and then our contact person told us to follow him to the cafeteria.

When we arrived at the cafeteria, everything got more human. We ordered some food and joined people sitting at a large table. As we ate, our contact person was having an unusual discussion with other personnel at the table.

The talk was all about making a decent living once they were out of military service, since their military service didn't prepare them for civilian jobs. Some thought they were going to be forced out of the military. Several had intended to stay on until retirement, but new directives from the White House made that impossible.

After we finished our food and drinks we walked back to our truck and found they had almost finished the unloading. We wanted to check out our trailer, but the security guards got nervous. I explained that we needed to contact our dispatcher.

We were escorted to a telephone in the next hallway, and every move we made was carefully observed. I saw some people going to a window in the hallway where they bought patches and insignia for their uniforms. I asked if I could purchase a souvenir as a reminder of our delivery. The guard said to go ahead but not a step past that window. I decided that the patches were too expensive for me.

Jinny and I were again standing at the back of our trailer when it became clear what all the heavy security was about. We watched people pushing a large cart that was transporting a nuclear bomb! It was yellow, with stabilizer fins on its tail. Symbols for radiation were plastered on it.

We stood absolutely still as this yellow baby was rolled past us.

Afterwards, we went outside and found a small area where some lawn chairs were sitting on a patio. A couple of military people came over and sat down near us. We had been watching the jets take off and land. One of the men said that the pilots were in training and he was an instructor. They were really doing some pretty neat flying, with sharp maneuvers.

I asked why I was seeing uniforms from other countries here. I was told that foreign military air force pilots are trained at this base—for a good fee. Wichita Falls is a great training spot because its weather is good most of the time.

We finally got an emptied trailer very late in the day. I pulled the trailer to the outside of the building's barrier fence before I closed its doors. Our contact person thanked us for being so patient, and then led us back out to the main gate of the base.

Maybe we weren't supposed to see anything, but we learned a lot.

Our Cat, Chester, Rides Along

Virginia Logan

One March we came home for dentist appointments and found our cat Chester a sick boy. We rushed him to the animal hospital. After several days and many tests later, the vet explained that our cat had kidney failure and needed to be on medication and a special prescription diet.

That made Chester a very expensive cat, so we decided to try taking him along with us in the big truck. Our company does allow animals in the trucks, although it's usually a dog. So Chester came along. We gave him the meds, and he got better. He seemed to like trucking and we enjoyed him, so he rode with us from that point on.

When we are stopped at night, if even for only a few hours, he took over the driver's seat!

Chester, our trucking companion

In May we experienced a very unusual solar halo. We were
waiting for a reload
in San Jose, Califor-
nia, when we heard
an excited caller on
the radio show we
were listening say,
"Go outside and
look up." It was
absolutely beauti-
ful.

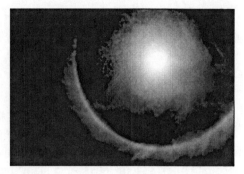

The San Jose Mercury described what we saw:
"The four-hour show began about 10 a.m. when
feathery cirrus clouds formed ice crystals at
about 30,000 ft and began acting like billions
of tiny prisms. Usually perceived on the ground
as a faint doughnut of yellow-orange light around
the sun, the halo that formed Tuesday instead
looked more like a completely round rainbow.

Orange, blue and red highlights attracted attention
all over the Bay Area. Meteorologists explained that
the temperature has to be just right for it to form
and that while a ring around the moon or sun can
signal a coming storm front, Tuesday's halo heralded
nothing more than high cloudiness."

In June and July we hauled many loads of onions from California back to Michigan. One particular reload in Arvin, California
stands out. We arrived early in the morning at the location, iden-
tified by the large stand of oleander bushes along the road.

There were a couple of small buildings and equipment for the field, but no loading docks.

When we asked where we were going to load, they pointed to the row in the field where we were to start. We drove 3 miles up and down the rows for 5 hours while the field hands threw the bags of onions up into the trailer and stacked them. It's usually about 800 bags to make a load so that was a long hot day.

That's what might be called a 'cheap hand operation.'

Driving our truck through the onion field

Nuke Load

John Logan

One of the more unusual truck loads ever hauled by the Logan team started out with a 'call at once' message from Jenny in our dispatch department. She said our next shipper wanted to run a background check on both Jinny and I before loading. This load was going to be very sensitive and needed careful handling.

We called the shipper in Napa, California, and gave the company owner all of our personal information. The shipper told us how to find him and also said we should be ready to load and get going quickly and quietly.

As it turned out this load was going to be worth millions of dollars. That's right, 'millions.'

By the time we arrived at Napa, California and were backed into the building, all of the FBI checks on us had been run. The next step was working out cargo liability insurance on this load. Then we got an eyeball on what we were to be hauling. It turned out to be machinery of a very special kind.

Every nuclear reactor in the world is supposed to have a piece of machinery that will shut the reactor down if something goes wrong. This machine must be as failsafe as man can make it and must work even if all the technicians are dead in the control room. These machines protect the general population if there is an accident or attack from unfriendly forces.

Our Federal Government, FBI, CIA, Nuclear Regulatory Commission and local utility people are very concerned about unfriendly forces that might seize or blow up one of our nuclear generating plants. These machines are one result.

When we got three large machines and a couple of small ones loaded into our trailer, they nearly filled it up. We were asked by the company owner to say nothing to anyone along the way about what we were hauling.

I asked why we were taking these machines to power generators that were already in operation, and was told that an accident had happened and, as a result, these machines had been completely rebuilt.

This shipper in Napa is one of only two companies in the entire world that do such repair work.

We started out from the shipper very late in the day, so we didn't get over the mountains before dark and had to change drivers when we reached the Nevada state line. We decided to grab a bite before continuing eastbound. I put two locks on the trailer doors in addition to the hardened seals that were fastened on the doors for security. I also left the trailer and tractor sitting in the light.

Once we had eaten, we really started to make some miles. Loaded as we were, it would be possible to do about 1,200 miles a day. If we stayed with it we should be able to reach our first stop in just one and a half days. That was at the Quad-Cities Nuclear Generating Station situated just north of I-80, on the bank of the Mississippi River.

We had given them our time of delivery and they were waiting for us. I discovered they had been watching us on cameras from the moment that we parked the truck on their property.

When the time for delivery arrived, I walked to the security headquarters building. They asked me to get the other driver, since we both had to turn over our license and answer all their questions about our personal histories. They checked us for contraband and put us inside a large X-ray and radioactive-materials detector.

While these people were checking us, they had a specialist checking our tractor and trailer, looking for drugs, guns, explosives, or any other items that could be used in an attempt to sabotage their nuclear machinery.

These people were well trained. We were introduced to a fellow who kept an eagle eye on us the entire time we were in the area. When we were cleared to drive into the property, he climbed right up into the truck and rode with us.

Once we got inside the plant boundary fence, we were not allowed to get down out of the truck, even to use a bathroom. I did have to get out to take care of my equipment and to check the other shipments still in the trailer. I was escorted and watched the whole time.

The guard watching us asked, "Do you see that line of large steel posts with large diameter cables strung between them?" He said that the threat of a terrorist attack on a nuclear generator required them to put up a barricade that even a military tank could not breach.

I found out what had happened to the machinery which had come from this site before it had been rebuilt. It seems that a janitorial person was assigned the duty of cleaning the cement floor upon which these machines had been sitting. He or she wanted to do a good job and get that cement floor as clean as possible. So that janitor poured some muriatic acid on the floor to get it extra clean.

Fumes from the acid had gotten inside these delicate machines and started to eat away at some of the electrical connections within the shut-down equipment. That made this very expensive equipment unreliable, so it was sent back to the builder for a complete rebuild job.

After we were finished, resealed and locked up, it was time for us to be on the way to the second power plant. Before we were allowed to leave we had to go through a special machine to see if we had been contaminated while on the property. The machine found no radioactivity. We were given our driver's licenses back along with our other identification. I was glad to be out of that restricted property and on my way again.

To say that this was an educational experience would be an understatement. Those people are ready for any eventuality or persons that might threaten that nuclear facility.

Our final stop was to be at a nuclear power plant located at Morris, Illinois. We were now running a little late. Jinny called the receiver and took directions on our cell-phone so we could keep moving while she talked.

At that time, the state of Illinois only allowed a truck to run a maximum of 55 mph. We kept at it and got to Morris just before our deadline. However, the consignee had neglected to tell us that his plant was only one among several in the area. Edison Electric owns a large amount of land in the Morris, Illinois area.

We found the wrong plant the first time around, but the actual delivery was a breeze. No security checks. We backed up to the receiving dock and zip-bang-boom, we were empty. I closed the doors and we got on our way quickly.

Rainbow and Her Dumpbucket

Virginia Logan

In April, we had delivered a load of books in Weaverville, North Carolina, and our message from dispatch was to relax and watch our satellite receiver. That means they have nothing yet and will be working on a reload.

So we returned to the truck stop at Chandler, North Carolina, just west of Ashville, and got some sleep!

At 2 p.m. our satellite beeped with a message to call the broker. We had a load to pick up in Kings Mountain, North Carolina and we had to be there no later than 4 p.m. That gave us just two hours to drive 105 miles over mountains.

We picked a route that looked best, which took us past a 'gem and gold mining camp.' It also had some of the most beautiful blooming dogwood trees we have ever seen. We planned to take Highway 74 right to Kings Mountain.

When I tried to call for directions on our cell phone, I got an operator that could not recognize our Cellular One phone. I tried to call 1-800 Call ATT, but with no luck. We knew if we got off the highway to find a phone, we would not make the 4 p.m. deadline. As a last resort, we got on our CB and asked for local information.

'Rainbow in her Dumpbucket' was the person who answered. She was going to KMG Minerals and said that we could just follow her. After many stop lights, we found Rainbow and followed her as she turned on a two lane shortcut to KMG Minerals.

Her 'dumpbucket' was a Mack truck with a three-axle covered trailer for hauling heavy loads of sand and rocks. Black smoke poured out of her truck stacks as she ran at about 65 mph on a skinny two-lane road with a 35 mph speed limit. We had to follow and keep up to her pace.

At one point, Rainbow suddenly swerved and smoke rolled out from around all of her 22 tires. The next thing we saw was a gentleman on a lawn tractor by the side of the road with a look of terror on his face. It looked as if our friend had nearly hit a very slow-moving vehicle.

No one was hurt, so we continued to follow Rainbow and made it to KMG Minerals, found the loading dock and got filled up with bags of special 'exotic metal casting sand.'

We said 'thanks' and headed for Detroit.

Blizzards & Hyakutake

Virginia Logan

January 1996 started on the southern edge of that year's big blizzard. We were driving I-85 from Atlanta, Georgia to Young-ville, North Carolina, where we had a Sunday morning pick-up of 5 pallets from an industrial park. Destination: Allegan, Michigan.

The industrial park was not plowed and the dock was situated so that our truck had to back around a curve and uphill to the dock. We got stuck! The employee who'd come to help us load called a friend with a wrecker. But the driver of the wrecker indicated that he didn't know what to do.

We had already figured out how we were going to execute the docking maneuver, so John explained what we needed to get back on the pavement. With a few pulls in the right direction, our truck was back on pavement and we got to the dock.

After loading, we began the long, nerve-wracking trip back north. I-77 north of I-40 was closed because of blowing snow, so we made our way to I-75. Because of icy roads and blowing snow, we cut our driving time to 4 hours each.

As we approached Cincinnati, Ohio about 7 a.m. the next morning, we heard that all local roads had been closed, with drivers getting a hefty fine if they were caught on them. We went on past and, despite the snow, reached Allegan, Michigan.

All this for 5 pallets of plastic bottles!

The next blizzard was in Nebraska. We drove as far as Grand Island, Nebraska in white-out condition, then stopped at Bossel-man's Truck Stop. We made a parking place facing east, with the wind howling out of the north. Within an hour we were surrounded by trucks parking anywhere they could 'put it down.'

By midnight, John discovered that the engine was trying to quit. We put on jackets, hats and gloves to get out and check things over—and found that the snow was up to our waist around the truck.

John got in front to pull the hood up and fell back into a snow bank. So much snow was blowing that it was difficult for us to breathe. The same was true for the truck. We discovered that the air filter was choked with snow and ice. We cleaned it out the best we could. That kept the engine going and kept us warm until morning, when the wind finally stopped blowing.

It was a stressful night with the wind rocking the truck. We couldn't try to go inside because we needed to stay aware of the air filter's condition. Also, our cat, Chester, couldn't stay out in the cold.

In the morning, trucks were jammed in everywhere and no one could move. The Truck Stop got two front-end loaders busy, so one-by-one the trucks got un-stuck and moved. Our truck and trailer had so much snow around and under it that we had to have the loader pull us out of our spot so we could get on our way.

One of the highlights of this year was viewing the comet 'Hyakutake' (named after the Japanese man who first spotted it). It was visible from March 16 through April 12, with the best views on March 24th and 25th.

On March 22nd, we left Holland, Michigan for San Jose, California, so we would be traveling I-80 across Wyoming on the evening of March 25th. We stopped in western Wyoming early in the evening at a parking area away from lights of truck stops or town.

We got out our binoculars to start searching the skies for this comet. Because of its tail, we spotted it without the binoculars.

We stopped again just before Wells, Nevada at Pequope, and took another look at the skies. At this point the comet was huge, with its tail spread across the whole sky!

NASA image of
Hyakutake

We were filled with awe and wonder. But it was also extremely cold, so we didn't linger long staring at the sky.

John at the
Ocean

Niece Nancy and husband Brent
visit with us in Tucson, Arizona

Virginia with her truck

Calling it Quits

Virginia Logan

After seven years of driving without accidents, and only one ticket (that Nevada fuel-sticker problem), we decided we'd treasure our record and call it quits.

In our last year, we'd carried tables for a new Bingo Hall at the Soaring Eagle Casino in Mount Pleasant, Michigan; a load of oil-dry to be used at the Charlotte Motor Speedway at Charlotte, North Carolina; a load of furniture to Universal City, California, that was to be used for a TV commercial (we backed our truck into a sound stage right next to 'Jurassic Park').

Over the years, we had hauled amazing amounts of the goods that are daily parts of American life. We carried:

- office furniture;
- apples & onions, coke syrup and chili powder;
- copy machines and drums of paint;
- egg cartons and dog food paper bags;
- iron castings and ceramic tiles from Mexico;
- computers, AC Units and conveyer systems;
- bulk mail, boxes of wine and whiskey;
- raw rubber, oil products, and cotton bales;
- books and DVD or VCR 'to be released' films;
- oriental rugs and Mississippi flood relief supplies.

For me the years of truck-driving were, overall, good ones. I learned how to adapt to a whole different lifestyle and enjoyed the brief insights into local culture. John really enjoyed seeing bald eagles, golden eagles, antelope, elk, mountain goats, caracara birds, and so many differently beautiful landscapes and water views. An experience like cross-country truck-driving expands your viewpoint.

We both enjoyed brief visits with John's brothers and his father on the West Coast. And we enjoyed sharing parts of our experience with our children, Marie and Jason.

The 24/7 togetherness also prepared us for the togetherness of retirement. Constant companionship can be stressful, especially when the demands of dispatchers, brokers, and deadlines are added to driving situations that are pressures in themselves.

We were grateful to have a home we could come back to, even for just a few days. We would feel like getting to Chicago was 'almost back home.'

Best of all, given many near-accidents, we survived. We think we'll enjoy staying home to watch storms on TV!

Headed into mountain snow, Coalville, Utah

On I-15 past St George, Utah, the road goes through a little
corner of Arizona before heading down into Nevada. This is the
Virgin River Gorge, a beautiful and challenging route to drive.
— Virginia Logan

CPSIA information can be obtained at www.ICGtesting.com
Printed in the USA
LVOW101340110612

285529LV00001BA/57/P